God's Fingerprints

GOD'S FINGERPRINTS
A Story of a Pastor's Son

Alfonso Gomez and David Rocha

PARAKLETOS PUBLISHING
MODESTO

God's Fingerprints Copyright © 2019 by Alfonso Gomez. All Rights Reserved.

Contents

Genesis 12:1-3 (NIV) 1
Foreword 3
Introduction 7
Disclaimer 9

1. The Beginning 10
2. Preacher's Kid 17
3. Frank's Shoes 23
4. Juvenile Hall 27
5. The Truck That Changed Everything 37
6. The Vision Once Again 41
7. The Plane Ride to Colombia 51
8. The Conference 55
9. 36 Chairs 65
10. Bloody Red Dirt 75
11. Coming Home 81
12. Brazil 89
13. The Promise 99

Epilogue 104
Philippians 1:6 (NIV) 111
Photo of chairs 113

Dedication 115
Thank You 117
Future 119
Contact 121

GENESIS 12:1-3 (NIV)

1 The Lord had said to Abram, "Go from your country, your people and your father's household to the land I will show you. ² "I will make you into a great nation, and I will bless you; I will make your name great, and you will be a blessing.
³ I will bless those who bless you, and whoever curses you I will curse; and all peoples on earth will be blessed through you."

Alfonso Gomez and David Rocha

FOREWORD

It is mind boggling what God can do in a person's life. I laugh at myself as I write this. I never imagined myself having anything to do with God, let alone, writing the foreword in a book that is about God. I never read a book until I was twenty years old. Yet today I love to read. I just finished reading this book that you now hold in your hands. I can tell you this, you're in for an adventure. But the cool thing about this adventure is that it is not made up. It is a true story about a real God, moving in the lives of real people, with real problems, and changing them, in a very real way! I cannot lie. Tears fell from my eyes more than once. I found myself with face in hands as I absorbed the things that I read. It was a roller coaster ride of emotions as it spoke right into my heart.

As you read, I know you'll be happy that you did. You might even find yourself finishing this book a different person than the one you were when you first began. There is only one way to find out, right?

I've heard people say that God has a sense of humor. In the past, I wouldn't have known what that meant, but today I do. God has a way of revealing Himself to people, especially those that doubt Him. Deep down inside you might be thinking, 'Yeah, that kind of stuff never happens to me.' Well let me tell you, I don't believe that it is an accident that you're reading these words. God knows exactly what He is doing. I pray you are willing to open your heart and ask Him to reveal Himself to you right now. Even if you're not ready right now, maybe these words of an old pastor of mine might speak to you.

"God hears the words of our heart long before He ever hears the words that come out of our mouth."

Powerful words. Encouraging words. These words have always stuck with me. I believe them because God has answered the silent prayers of my heart time and time again. God is more than real, He is active and listening to us even when we aren't speaking. He hears our hearts. Knowing this, it gives me hope. I pray it gives you hope also! It's one thing to believe that God exists, but it is quite another to believe that He actually cares and is willing to get involved in our lives.

The bible talks about God using the most unlikely people to carry out His purposes, but I never would've thought that God could or would use someone like me. If you had known me before I knew Christ, you might've thought there was no way that I would be a Christian. God had other plans for me. I've had the opportunity to serve the Lord in several capacities. The Lord has allowed me to be a youth pastor, an assistant pastor, and even the lead pastor of a church. I still laugh that God would take a guy like me and turn my life around for the good. These days, I go into the county jail and minister to the men that are locked up. My entire goal is to remind the inmates that God is not finished with them. He has a calling and a purpose for their lives. There is hope. Not one person is so far gone that God cannot reach them.

Look at what the bible has to say:

"Brothers and sisters, think of what you were when you were called. Not many of you were wise by human standards; not many were influential; not many were of noble birth. But God chose the foolish things of the world to shame the wise; God chose the weak things of the world to shame the strong. God chose the lowly things of this world and the despised things—and the things that are not—to nullify the things that are, so that no one may boast before him." – 1 Corinthians 1:26-29

This is one of my favorite scriptures. It reminds me. No matter where a person is at in life, or how far off course it may appear they are, that God is at work! God is calling men and women even while walking in darkness. The Lord is unstoppable. No matter how difficult the situation may be, the Lord is more than able to break through and prove that He is the final word. People may wrestle with God but it's much too hard to resist His love. He takes hard hearts and makes them new. He did it for me, and He can do it for you.

When my friend David Rocha introduced me to Alfonso at House of Rest Church, I instantly knew I was speaking with somebody with a heavy calling on his life. Alfonso spoke to me about some of the things that the Lord has put on his heart and his reason for wanting to share his testimony through this book that he and David would be publishing called, "God's Fingerprints." Something inside of me knew that this was something that needed to go out for others to hear. I know it's going to impact many lives.

I could see the compassion in Alfonso's eyes and his heart came through as he shared with me his concern not only for those that don't know the Lord but also for those that do know Him yet don't follow Him. It is my hope and prayer that the Lord uses this book to minister to you and brings about a radical change in the way you see yourself and others. God is an awesome God, and with Him all things are possible!

Carlos Garcia
Hanford, California

INTRODUCTION

God's promises are guaranteed on His time. You might be going through something in your life right now. Problems or situations arise, and you don't understand why. I would like to remind you of something. God has a purpose for you. Even through the struggles, He will still make it profitable for building your character, and for His Glory. God's promises will reach you. Not in your time, but in His time.

Alfonso Gomez and David Rocha

DISCLAIMER

Parental warning: Some material in this book might not be suitable for all audiences. It can be strong content for some readers.

THE BEGINNING

ALFONSO GOMEZ AND DAVID ROCHA

My name is Alfonso Gomez, and this is my story. In writing this, I didn't quite know where to begin, because I quickly realized that I needed to, in a sense, set the stage. So many things were happening around the world, and especially in the United States during this time. Allow me to set the foundation for what life was like in the early 1980s for a young Latino growing up in northern California. Ronald Reagan was elected President of the United States in 1981, and this brought one of the most aggressive policies on the 'war on drugs.' It was sweeping across the nation. Thus, creating a culture within a culture known as the cholo lifestyle. Mexican Americans that had a certain way to dress, a certain slang, and pride that rivaled those in military ranks. It was like a giant black cloud that I had no idea was about to hover over the fields and small towns of the central valley. Prison gang wars were erupting behind the walls and the politics of it was about to explode in the streets, leaving pools of blood and bullet casings across many neighborhoods in the central valley of California.

In looking back, I believe that I was born into a very broken family. It was 1982 and we lived in the projects of west side Modesto. I am not sure how it happened, but one day a woman shared the gospel of Jesus Christ with my mom. This was a big problem, culturally speaking because my dad and mom came from a long line of Catholics that dated back generations. Yet, even amid this, my mom accepted Jesus Christ into her heart and became a Christian. Knowing that my dad would have never allowed it. My mom followed Christ in secret and could never fellowship or go to a Christian church. Yet, even though she herself could never go to a church, she would send my older half-brother to the church by lying to my dad. She would tell him that he was going to visit his aunt that lived in Modesto, yet the entire time he was in a Christian church service each Sunday. She was afraid that my dad would have rejected her, or maybe even kill her. Not much time passed that her confession to follow Christ and be a Christian would be out in the open. Her entire family turned their back on her. I realize now the huge price she paid to follow her heart in serving Christ outside of the Catholic church.

Two years had passed with my mom as a Christian and my dad wanting nothing to do with her Christianity, her church, her pastors or her 'hallelujahs'. They had moved out of Modesto and went a few miles south on Highway 99 to the small town of Turlock. We lived in a small apartment in a predominately Chicano and Mexican neighborhood. I have early memories of my dad and uncles drinking alcohol and hanging out. I am not saying the apartment was a mess, but when I think back, I remember beer cans and trash. One of my uncles was cartel *mafioso* related and was very tough and violent. Eventually, he was sent to federal prison for eight years for drug trafficking. Then deported back to Mexico after serving his sentence in federal prison.

July 7, 1984, is a day my mom will never forget. The marriage was falling apart. I believe my mom felt that the end was coming near for the family. What she didn't know was that my dad was planning to walk out on her and the entire family for good that day. He was literally getting ready in the bathroom to leave with my uncle and go to Tijuana Mexico. I believe it was out of desperation for her family, so she decided to invite the pastors over to speak to my dad. She was afraid and had no idea on how he would react. Was he going to flip out? Was he going to walk out on them? I believe she was brave and found the strength within herself because it was God's appointed time. When the pastors knocked on the door and she let them in, it was as if all time stood still. One of the pastors, named Jose, played a major role in my story years later. I wholeheartedly believe that the talk was more than just bible verses because my dad wouldn't have sat down to hear a sermon. Even though I wasn't in the room. I believe that the words from the pastor's mouth were orchestrated by the Lord Himself, because my dad sat down with them and allowed the pastor to speak. So, when my dad sat there with these men, something began to tug at his heart. The pastor asked my dad if he could pray for him, and my dad said "Yes." I don't know what words he said in his prayer, but it shook everything within my dad. From the stories I have heard about my dad, it was amazing that he even allowed them to pray for him. And it was there, in my small kitchen, that my dad accepted and surrendered his life to Jesus Christ.

During the prayer of salvation, my dad has told me countless times of the vision the Lord gave him at that very moment. As his eyes were shut, with the prayer of the pastor in his ears, he saw two giant hands reach into his heart. The giant hands began to pull out dead blackbirds and filled multiple garbage cans with them. It was a vision that was so vivid, so real, so moving, that to this day he still remembers it as if it just happened. In that very moment, in the small kitchen of my home, my dad changed and became a new man. Old things had passed away and all things became new. His heart of stone was ripped out of his chest, and God put a new heart into him. My dad became a Christian. My dad knew nothing about the Bible, yet God gave him a vision, a purpose, and a call. What happened that day was something only God Himself could do. He felt free for the first time in his life and has never looked back.

From that day on, everything changed within the household. My mom and dad began to reconcile their marriage. He began to seek holiness in his life and in his family. My mom is the first believer between them both, saw my dad reach toward God in a way that she never imagined. They began living a Christian life together and laid a foundation for the entire family. Up until that point, my mom was living on simple faith. She wasn't allowed to go hear sermons, or attend prayer groups. Now with my dad leading the family in the ways of Christ, she was now free to grow in her walk in the Lord. After six months I still remember moving from Turlock back to Modesto. My parents purchased their first home and began regularly attending a church. This created new friends and family that would come to our home for fellowship. I still remember the peace that was over our home, people came with their bibles to discuss, pray and fellowship. I didn't quite understand the situation, but what I did know is that things were a whole lot better in our home than it was before.

Within months my dad began pastoring a small church in Salida, on the outskirts of Modesto, without having any bible college certification, degree, or credentials. My dad is a very smart intellectual man. I realize now that God had been preparing my dad years before he surrendered his life to the Lord. So many people think that God begins to prepare a man or a woman once conversion happens. That is so far from the truth. Everything we do in life, in our youth, in our childhood, and in our adult lives are already led by God to shape us into who we are truly meant to be once we come to Christ.

The small church began with six to eight members. Within one year, it had grown to one hundred members. By this time my dad had enrolled in a Bible Institute and at the same time he was pastoring, he was also learning about God and the Scriptures. I still remember being excited as he would walk into the house with a button-down shirt and tie. My siblings and I would run to him and I still recall feeling so proud of him. I wasn't accustomed to seeing him dressed up. Up to that point in my life, he was a cannery worker and laborer.

After some time, my dad came home and was in his room in prayer. He hadn't seen a vision from God since the day he surrendered his life to Christ. My dad was never the type of man to have visions from God, nor was he the type of man to say that God spoke to him in visions. I was now five years old. And on this evening, the Lord allowed my dad to see a vision for each of his kids. Myself, and my siblings. My dad to this day has not seen all these visions come to fruition, but he continues to believe what the Lord showed him that day so many years ago. In the vision he had about me, I was already grown and standing in Colombia, South America. I was wearing a white shirt with a bible in hand and I was yelling out, *"Colombia para Cristo"* (Colombia for Christ.) As soon as he saw these visions for each of us, he quickly reached for a pad of paper and began to write them down in detail. It is so important that when God gives us a Word, a vision or a dream. We document it, write it down in a journal and date it. I would like to make a note here to mention that I am not Colombian, nor are my parents. My dad had never been to Colombia and didn't have any ties to anyone of Colombian descent. Both sides of my family are Mexican, and I am a first-generation American. Growing up I knew nothing of or much less heard of Colombia. As the years passed and my dad would continually speak to me about this vision and calling for my life, I thought he was crazy. As far as I knew, Colombia was on another planet. Yet my dad continually spoke the vision into my life, as well as the vision he had for each of my siblings.

In looking back to that time, it was 1985 when my dad was given the vision of reaching Colombia for Jesus. Since then, this has made me look at history and what was happening in Colombia during those same years. I was shocked to see that it was the peak of the Pablo Escobar cartel. Eleven judges and 90 other people were killed by M-19 guerillas who invaded the Palace of Justice. Murder was at an all-time high in Colombia. And during the upheaval that was happening in that country, the Lord gives a vision to a praying pastor, my dad. A vision of me, in that far away country, yelling out *"Colombia para Cristo"*. God came to save humanity, and the blood that was spilling in that country was crying out for the Savior of this world. How beautiful are the feet of those that preach the gospel.

2

PREACHER'S KID

It was now 1990 and the west side neighborhood of Modesto was infested with gangs and drugs. Shootings, stabbings, and murders were taking place continually. I remember watching my older brother playing around, pretending to get jumped into a gang as a joke by neighborhood friends. It was during this time that my dad was led to pastor a church in Manteca, California. Roughly twenty minutes north of Modesto. It was a small group that had been gathering weekly but did not have a pastor. Soon after we moved to Manteca, I was eleven years old at the time. By this time, I was influenced by the things that I saw at school and in the streets. I also had an uncle that was in and out of jail. He was affiliated with the mafiosos in Mexico. His son, my cousin, lived with us since my uncle was living a reckless lifestyle and couldn't take care of him. Meeting the people at the new church was good and I was able to meet other young people that were my age and their families. I still remember the first guy I met. He was standing outside smoking a cigarette and wearing a heavy metal shirt. Then I met Ricky, who to this day is still my best friend. I found myself in a double life. Raised in a Christian home, yet at the same time, the street lifestyle was like a magnetic force, pulling me further and further away from all that was good.

After a couple of years, my uncle was released from incarceration and rented an apartment in Turlock, Ca. (Which is roughly an hour south from Manteca.) So even though my dad was raising his brother's son, my uncle would come each weekend to pick both of us up. I was now thirteen years old and I thought my uncle was the coolest guy around. He was tough and always carried guns. Things young boys like myself liked. To my dad, it looked as if my uncle had gotten his life together. In the beginning, he would come by and just leave money for my dad to help in raising his son. Over time, after my dad seeing this. He convinced him to be a bigger part of his son's life. To this present day, my dad has no idea that as soon as I would get in the car with my cousin to leave, that everything would change. His way of talking, his demeanor was still the same as he was before his incarceration. My cousin and I were only eight months apart. I was very close to him and to my uncle.

One day, my uncle came to pick me up in his Lincoln Town car. On this specific weekend, my cousin was already at his apartment with him, but I wanted to go also. So, when he picked me up in his big gangster Lincoln Town Car, *corridos* were playing loudly on his stereo. *Corridos* were Mexican folk songs with violent and drug-related lyrics. These music artists would make songs about famous drug kingpins and each song was more violent than the last one. As we pulled away from my driveway, he reached into his pants and pulled out a bag of cocaine. It was my first-time doing drugs, and it was my uncle that exposed me. Once we arrived at his apartment, he asked me if I wanted marijuana, cocaine or prostitutes. He had no hesitation or remorse in exposing his young thirteen-year-old nephew or son to these things. By this time, my cousin would guard his dad's drugs at the apartment when my uncle was gone in case someone would try to break in.

One time while at the apartment, we were getting high and sitting in the living room. My uncle would be drinking and began talking about murders and crimes that he had done to people. It was like torture for my cousin and me to hear these stories because we had known some of the people. To this day, I don't know why my uncle would show me a big bag of coke and allow me to try it. I liked the excitement of it all and I understood that there was a gangster world out there, a crime life that people lived out. At this point of my life, I already understood that my uncle was involved in this crazy fast lifestyle, yet it was a complete contrast with my dad sitting at home with his nose in the bible. It was boring to me. Home represented a boring life. A Christian home, going to church, people coming over for fellowship. For a teenager during this time, it was so much better to be around my uncle. I began to see the influence and power that drugs had when one sold them. It was a very dark and evil world and I was falling in headfirst.

Even though my uncle would offer things to me, and say "Whatever you want nephew, it is done".

I was still a thirteen-year-old boy, so I would decline the prostitutes and hard drugs. What I did want was marijuana. My uncle offered me a deal. We were sitting down in his apartment and he began to talk to me.

He said, "Your buddies are going to smoke weed anyway, you might as well make money off of them."

I didn't fully understand the hustle at that time.

He continued to tell me, "Look...I got pounds," and he showed me a stash of multiple pounds of marijuana.

Then he said, "I can bring you two pounds on Sunday, but you need to stay home on that day when your dad goes to church. I will give them to you for $700 each. We can do this every other week."

Soon after that, I woke up on a Sunday morning and pretended to be sick. Other Sundays after that I would wake up late, get ready late, so my dad would leave without me to church. As soon as my dad would leave, I would communicate with my uncle and he would come over in his old orange van and drop off two bricks of weed to me. I began hustling marijuana. I had acquired a small hand-held scale and broke the pounds down into ounces. I would carry two ounces in each of my socks and would try to move them at school. To be honest, I was never a good drug dealer, even though I tried. Now as I look back, I often wonder if my uncle exposed me to these things to create another cash flow for himself. Maybe part of it was he thought he was doing me a favor by teaching me the game. Another possibility was through myself and my cousin, he wanted to create a crime family. I was very afraid of my uncle and when it came time to pay him, I felt that he would have killed me if I didn't have all the money. Sometimes I would let them take weed without paying me upfront, then when it came the time to pay, they never paid me. A few times I had to borrow money from my older brother because he worked at McDonald's and I feared the repercussions.

My life began to really take a turn for the worst. Cocaine use, smoking weed, selling weed, and as if nothing could get any worse, the street gang culture began to sweep through California like wildfire. For me, it began at my dad's church, and because he was a Hispanic minister, he would preach in Spanish. So that brought along many first-generation Mexicans that fluently only spoke Spanish. Within the same church were Mexican families that had been in the United States for generations. So, the youth of the church began to bang *Sur* which is short for *Sureno* or southerner. And the English-speaking youth began to bang *Norte*, which means a northerner from Northern California.

This became a major issue in the early 1990s in the cities and towns of California. In prisons across the state, lines were being drawn between Mexicans from Southern California and Northern California. Prison riots erupted, and many individuals began to murder each other over who controlled the prison and the drug trade within it. Over time this war within the walls leaked out into the neighborhoods and destroyed families. Northern convicts were outnumbered in the California prison system, and the best way to grow in number was to recruit youngsters in their very own neighborhoods back home.

So here I am, being forced to choose a side, along with most of the youth in my dad's church. At one time we were all friends, now there was a line of separation in the youth, and this began to spill out onto the streets of Manteca Ca.

FRANK'S SHOES

I want to mention how the gang lifestyle directly affected our life in my dad's church. As I was growing up, along with the youth into our teenage years, it became a serious problem. The tension of street issues became a regular thing during church services. There was constant friction from the street into the sanctuary. These were the same youth that grew up together as friends. There were two specific kids that really brought the street life into my circle of influence during that time. And unfortunately, it was during this time that one of the youths in my dad's church was involved in the murder of another of the youth, named Frank. Both families, of the killer and the killed, attended my dad's church. This caused a huge rift in the church and the family of the killer completely stopped attending. This was the first time anyone from my dad's congregation had ever passed away, much less murdered. This was the first funeral that my dad was asked to officiate. This was one of the first murders in Manteca that happened due to gangs.

Before the funeral, my dad asked Frank's family for a pair

of his shoes. He wanted to preach at the funeral, with the sermon, 'What are you going to do with Frank's shoes.' During the funeral, my dad was holding them up in the air. Every single gang member and wanna-be gang banger was in the audience. My dad saw this as an opportunity to preach the gospel to each gang member that attended. To this day everyone that was there remembers the powerful message that my dad spoke.

Frank was one of the toughest gang members I knew in all of Manteca. He was the type to never back down from anyone. He was well respected and feared. I would have feared him myself, but we grew up together at my dad's church. Frank was raised in the church. We participated in church activities, church plays, and other activities, along with other kids. Even the one that would later be a part of his murder.

One thing that most don't know about Frank is a conversation I had with him three days before he was killed. I had picked him up to go to the store and we were smoking a joint.

He sat right next to me and said, "Man bro... we should all go back to church. We should all start serving God. I'm sick and tired of being 'Chito', I want to be Frank... Can you take me to your dad's house so he can pray for me?"

Frank always considered my dad to be his pastor. We were completely high, so I didn't want to go see my dad in that condition.

I said, "I'll take you on another day."

The other day never came. Three days later he was

murdered. To this day, this haunts me. I replay that day in my mind and what I should have done. I should have taken him. I should have listened. Would he still be here to this day if I had just taken him?

JUVENILE HALL

When it happened, it was on a Wednesday night service and my dad was preaching. My little brother snuck out of the church and climbed a building. Then began throwing light bulbs from the building onto Main street and someone called the police. They arrested my brother outside and the police came into the church while my dad was preaching. They pulled him down from the pulpit to tell him that they were arresting his son. At this point, we were already affecting my dad's ministry and we were both completely out of control.

As a footnote, I do need to mention how much Hollywood films had and have a dangerous influence over the youth of this nation, including myself. In 1988, a movie titled 'Colors' hit theaters across the nation. It was a movie based on gangs in Los Angeles killing each other over red and blue, Blood and Crips and how the Los Angeles police department dealt with the gangsters. After this movie released, kids everywhere became infatuated with the gangster lifestyle. Matter of fact, on the opening day of the film in the city of Stockton, (10 minutes north of Manteca.) There was a long line of young people waiting to watch the film and a young man wearing blue was murdered by another young man wearing a red bandana. Because of this, the San Joaquin law enforcement banned the film in Stockton.

I still remember the introduction to the movie, showing two jail cells, one full of Bloods and the other full of Crips as both groups are throwing up gang signs and yelling to each other with a song by rapper Ice-T. I can still remember some of the lyrics of the song.

"I am a nightmare walking, psychopath stalking. King of the jungle just a gangster stalking. Living life like a firecracker, quick is my fuse. Vendettas of death by the colors I choose. Red or blue, Cuz or Blood, it just don't matter. Sucker dive for your life when my shotgun scatters. The gangs in L.A. will never die... just multiply. Colors."

Other films soon followed with the same type of influence, such as 'American Me', and 'Mi Vida Loca'. Also, an older film, yet just as influential was Blvd Nights. I sometimes wonder if the directors of these types of movies knew what they truly did to society, to California, the United States and eventually to the entire world. They released a spirit of destruction upon the world. They exposed, highlighted, and glorified the gangster lifestyle. It messed up society and entire generations. I understand that in Los Angeles there had been generations of gangs, but for the young people growing up in northern California, especially the small towns of the central valley, these movies had a major impact. Some gangsters might not admit that fact, but I remember after films like these, people began to mimic the clothes and the style in the streets.

I myself was never a gangbanger as far as claiming a specific neighborhood or gang. I honestly didn't want to be a part of the gang lifestyle. My biggest influence was my brothers. In a sense, I felt forced, because I was always going to back them up no matter what. This was the life they chose for themselves, so I went along. I wasn't so much defending the homies, I was defending my brothers.

This leads me to talk a bit about influence. The definition of influence: *the capacity to have an effect on the character, development, or behavior of someone or something, or the effect itself.* This is such a powerful word in the sense that we can actually lead a person to destruction or success. I don't know who is reading this book, but I would like to give you something to think about. Whether you realize it or not. Your actions, your choices are a direct influence on someone around you. It could be a brother or sister, a friend or co-worker. It can even be your own spouse. The enemy uses this influence that others have on others, to lead them down a dark spiral. This is the very reason Jesus came as a man. He came with a mission to not only save humanity but to be an example for us. To be an influence on how to live a righteous life. He came to have an effect on our character, development, and behavior. I believe that this is one of the enemy's biggest tools in his bag of tricks. He uses the influence of movie stars, rock stars, books, movies, and social media to influence not only the youth but the very nation itself. Whether you admit it to yourself or not, deep down you know exactly who you have influence with. I'll leave you with this question. Are you being responsible with the influence you carry over them? Or will their fall come at the cost of being influenced by you?

My very first time of being arrested was in nearby Tracy, Ca. I walked into a Quik Stop. I was on my way to Livermore to party. I thought it was a good idea to get some beer, even though I was too young to buy it. So here I am, walking into the store thinking it would be a piece of cake to do a beer run. There was no way the older store owner could catch me. I grabbed two cases of beer and quickly made my way to the door. Just as I make it past the door, a Tracy police officer pulls into the parking lot. I didn't know what to do, I was caught red-handed. I left my boys and ran into the nearby neighborhood. The officer was in pursuit and I am jumping as many fences as I can to get away. My heart is pounding, and I have no idea where to go. I came across a party with the backyard full of people. They begin to direct me on how to get away from the cops. I thought that was crazy, how bad must this neighborhood be if the entire block is helping me to get away? I finally settled in and hid under an RV, but the police eventually found me and took me to jail.

I was taken to Juvenile Hall in Stockton, Ca. Up to this point, gangs were just a fun thing, but at this place, it became real, very fast. I was nervous as I was being booked. I had heard so many stories of what happens in jail. My mind was reeling with so many thoughts, but they were quickly put to rest. Everyone already knew who I was, because of my younger brother's constant incarcerations. Inmates, officers, and counselors all knew my younger brother. He had a good street reputation which always put him in Unit 3, which was for high risk and violent inmates. After settling into my cell all night, I was awakened in the early morning. It was chow time. I had never been locked up, but I already knew that in jail you must sit with your own kind. As I made my way into the chow hall, I quickly scanned the entire room looking for, my people. I instinctively sat with fellow Nortenos and introduced myself. I still remember sitting with Franky from South Side Stockton and Tony from East Side Stockton. At this time, South Side Stockton and East Side Stockton were having so many problems and were constantly murdering each other. Yet here they were sitting together at the same table as homeboys. Everyone understood that once you were behind bars, neighborhood beefs took the back seat because first and foremost you were a homeboy. And it was here that I finally began to represent Manteca. I still remember one of the homies telling me, "When I get out in three days, I'm going to kill a rival." Three days after he was released, he was back for exactly that. He was now in for murder. I was impressed with the drive for the cause. I only knew him for three days, and he will never know the influence he had on my life. When he walked back in, he was treated like a hero. These guys were rough and tough and were leading the charge in this cultural war. They were holding it down inside the walls and I respected that. The influence of the movies made in my younger years was nothing compared to these real-life gangsters.

By the time I was eighteen years old, I had been to juvenile hall seven times and my brother had been locked up as a juvenile twenty-five times. Here we both were, the pastor's sons, completely out of control. My parents had no idea what to do with us. They both felt safer knowing that we were in jail than out on the streets. Most of my arrests were due to my own dad calling the police on me, then I'd be arrested for violation of probation. The officers would find marijuana in my possession. A few times it was drunken rages and fighting. There I was again, back behind bars. My mom would see us flamed up (wearing red) and worry that we would kill someone or be killed. Even though we were kids, the spirit of destruction was all over us. I began to hate my dad and mom because out of the seven times I was arrested, only three of them were for crimes, the other four arrests were because of them calling the police on me.

What is ironic is that my parents felt safer when we were locked up. Yet it was in the jail that the stakes of life and death were higher. I still remember one time I was in unit six, and I heard over the correctional officer's radio.

"Emergency in unit three, emergency in unit three!" and I could hear my younger brother yelling in the background, beating on a rival.

And I began saying, "That's my brother, that's my brother!"

Then later that same day, they transferred the guy to my

unit. I also assaulted him. I doubt he knew that both assaults were from two brothers.

In juvenile hall, I had a laundry job, which allowed me to go into unit three to see my brother. He was constantly in trouble, always on lockdown and banging every moment he was awake. By the time my brother was an adult, he had spent a combined four and half years behind bars as a juvenile. To this day he has no memories of a Christmas or birthday that he was out free.

My school life reflected the choices I was making. By the time I was a sophomore I was already a high school dropout. I began attending a continuation school along with my brother, but to me, it was a den of thugs that made things worse. Students were snorting meth in the classroom.

So here we are, being menaces to society and my dad continuing to pastor the church. One of the reasons I am writing this book is because many times, the pastor's kids are the worst kids. Maybe a pastor is reading this, and your situation isn't on this level, or maybe it's an even worse level. Maybe the pastor or leader reading this has a son or daughter that is completely lost or going in the wrong direction. So much is expected from your children because of who you are in the church. The reality is that there is a spiritual war going on. My dad was raising hell on the devil and because of this, the enemy trampled those closest to my dad's heart. I am a true believer that pastors risk their entire family when choosing to serve God. The church needs to continually pray and stand in the gap for the leaders in their lives. I don't claim to know it all. Maybe the church was praying for my dad but not us. I don't know. Maybe I will never know. Please take heed as I pray that this opens the eyes of those reading this book. Pastor, the enemy hates you and wants you to stop preaching the gospel. I am in no way telling you to stop or to be afraid but be vigilant. So many pastor's kids grow up in a homosexual lifestyle, porn addicts, drugs addicts, gangs, or maybe they aren't into any of those things and are achieving amazing things in a college, university or career. Yet they now reject the God that you preach. Maybe in a ministerial level, you are doing great and your ministry is successful, but your family is wrecked and falling apart. I just want to remind you that the devil wants to have a feast in destroying your family, but please never let it stop you from preaching Jesus from the mountaintops. *Greater is He that is in you than he that is in the world.*

I remember taking drugs to church and selling it to some of the youth. One thing I need to say is that even though my brother and I had completely fallen away from our Christian upbringing. We were both very different in the things that influenced us. For me, I was highly influenced by my drug dealing uncle. The fast life was enticing; Drugs, women, and power.

I remember once I told my brother to come to hang out with me, "I got girls! I got drugs!"

My brother would reply, "F*** drugs! F*** women! I just want to gangbang!"

That is all he wanted to do. Represent and hurt others

that didn't stand for what he stood for. In that sense, we were both going completely different directions.

One thing I need to say; Throughout this insane and crazy turbulent time in the life of our family, through my dad calling the police on me, the arguments, and the disappointments he had from my choices, my dad never stopped reminding me of the vision of me in Colombia. He would knock it into my head, speaking it into my mind that one day I would be in Colombia proclaiming Jesus to the people. He never visited me in jail, he didn't like seeing me there. But every time I would be released, I'd sit with him.

He would tell me, "Someday son, God showed me that you will never be the same."

I would tell him, "Dad, I know nothing about Colombia".

I didn't understand and thought my dad was crazy. I figured that he didn't know what he was talking about. If he truly knew my heart and the things in my mind, surely, he wouldn't be saying these things. Colombia was over two thousand miles away, what the heck was I going to be doing over there? The faith of my dad amazes me to this day. It reveals the character of his heart. I have learned over the years that my dad believed more in what God promised him over what he saw happening in the life of his family and those around him. Even through us destroying the youth at the church, disrupting ministry, going to jail, doing drugs, he still stood still in the promises of God. I don't know how he did it. He never fell off or fell away, and he never gave up on the promises. I am not saying he didn't get angry and frustrated at the situation, but the vision God gave him stayed stamped in the deepest parts of his heart.

5

THE TRUCK THAT CHANGED EVERYTHING

My teen years passed, and I was now a young adult. My oldest brother decided to join the United States Army. A situation occurred where my youngest brother robbed a house and stole some guns. Well, my older brother helped him to hide the weapons. And within a few days, he was arrested. So, in trying to help my older brother, an uncle came to speak to him and convinced him to join the army. There he was, on his way to boot camp. We decided to party before he left. The four of us bought two thirty packs of beer. We began drinking in the morning and had planned to have a good time all day before he left. My older brother loved to party. We knew he would be gone for six months to boot camp. Even though we started drinking in Manteca, by that night, we ended up in the city of Modesto at a club called the Firehouse. I had a fake ID, due to being under the age of twenty-one. The ID belonged to a forty-nine-year-old man. I didn't look like a gang banger, I would dress appropriately. As soon as I would pay to get into the club, I would spark a conversation and each time I would be let in. While in the club, my brother met some girls and decided to leave me. We had been drinking since the morning, so we're both out of our minds. I found myself outside trying to figure out how I was going to get home. Out of the corner of my eye, I see a work truck. I had no idea on how to steal cars, but the truck had a toolbox in the back. I grabbed a screwdriver and jammed it as hard as I could into the ignition. I forced it to turn and the truck engine started. I figured I would just drive it back to Manteca, so I could get home. I began driving completely drunk and forgot to turn the headlights on. I passed a patrol car going the opposite way and as soon as he passed me, he turned around and came behind me. He flashed his lights and I pulled over. Just as he gets out of the patrol car, I realize I am drunk and in a stolen car. I quickly put the car in drive and punched the gas all the way down. All I remember is flying through the west side of Modesto and hitting a brick wall. I wasn't wearing a seat belt so upon impact I bashed my mouth into the steering wheel. After the accident, I jumped out of the truck and fought with the police. I always resisted arrest. This was a huge crossroad in my life. If I hadn't gotten in that accident, I guarantee I would have ended up in prison or dead. This incident stopped me in my tracks. I didn't want to gang bang, I didn't want to do any more crimes, I didn't want to steal cars. I wanted to completely stop. The accident broke all my front teeth.

The next day I woke up in the men's adult county jail in horrible pain, not remembering what I did. I was now an adult, so I was not taken to juvenile hall. Just four months prior I was caught in a stolen car with a gun as a minor. I was not eighteen years old at that time. Now, here at the adult jail, I looked into the scratched shiny metal that is supposed to be a mirror and my teeth were completely broken. The county jail in Modesto is the closest thing you will ever get to know how a prison looks. It is built small, multiple floors with tiers of cells. It is loud all day and all night. Gang activity, yelling and hollering nonstop. I was completely reeling, confused and lost in this hell hole. My life was a mess. The police were making fun of me because of my missing teeth. They put my teeth in my wallet so when I was released on a later date, I would find them. I have personally witnessed police brutality.

One time I was injured, and the police were taking me to the hospital in handcuffs in the back seat, speeding eighty miles an hour on the freeway, then hitting the brakes so I would fly into the barricade in the middle of the car with my full weight. Police were doing very dirty things in those days and I personally experienced the wrath of that.

That same day after I woke up, my mom and my brother came to visit me in the county jail. The same brother that was leaving to boot camp and had left me at the club. I stayed in that county jail for four months, then I was transferred to the honor farm for two months. That was my only and last time that I ever went to adult jail. I did get arrested a few more times but I never caught a case that ended with my incarceration.

I lived a year without my teeth. I served my entire sentence with no teeth, and finally, my dad paid to reconstruct my mouth. One day while in jail, I still remember watching television one late night and the local news was showing my high school class of 1998 graduation ceremony. I was high on smoking weed and I sat there watching. Thinking to myself, 'I'm supposed to be there with them graduating. My life is a complete mess. Look at where I'm at, and these kids at the graduation are normal people. And here I am in jail.' I felt my heart drop, how did I become such a loser? A felon, with broken teeth sitting in jail, was not how I thought my life would end up.

By this point, my younger brother was still in and out of jail. I am in jail, my dad having so many issues at the church, and his sons being out of control didn't help the situation. My dad was asked to step down from pastoring and told to take care of his family. Unfortunately, things did not get any better. I stopped gang banging, but I got into a different type of life. Going to nightclubs in San Francisco, dancing, doing drugs, and running wild with women. I had girlfriends in different cities and getting women was never a problem for me. I was just doing my thing and living a fast life.

THE VISION ONCE AGAIN

Months passed by and I heard from a friend about some good work opportunities in the state of Alaska. After my jail sentence from the truck accident, I wasn't around my homies as much as before. I figured it would be good for me to get away and make some good money out of state. A friend approached me with the idea. He himself would leave for a few months and work on a crab fishing boat and come back with loads of cash. I respected this guy because he was a hustler. He had been doing this type of work for a few years. I guess after a while he became a recruiter and would get paid to find people to come out to work.

Another reason I wanted to leave California was that six-months prior to this opportunity, my younger brother was sentenced to eighteen years in state prison. I knew that if I stayed home that I would get into trouble. Besides my brother going to prison, a good friend was murdered. I just needed to get away. After signing up to go, I was on my way, all alone, to Alaska. When I arrived, I found out that I was going to share a small room with three other men. It was like a jail cell. I overlooked the situation because my intention was to make some money, change my life, work hard, and get away from California. I began working on the coast in giant boats that were operating as canneries. I wouldn't go out into the ocean to catch the crabs, but when the boats would come in they would bring them to our cannery boat. I worked twelve-hour days nonstop. I did this for three months.

One day, a friend invited me to his room and I couldn't believe it. He had a room all to himself and I saw that he was also into selling drugs. I quickly realized there was more going on than just working in the canneries and boats. Soon I found myself getting into fights, collecting money and being a muscle. I wasn't the toughest guy, but I wasn't afraid of anything. If something had to be handled, I would handle it. So here I am, out of California, yet the California lifestyle followed me. Before long, life became all about smoking weed, drugs, power, and women all over again. It was at this place that something a friend said made perfect sense. He said, "Alfonso, sometimes you can go into a world so dark that you can never come out of it the same." I hesitate at this part of my story because it is so shameful. To the point of exploiting a woman and losing my entire dignity just for the sake of power and money. It became the pinnacle of my life that caused years of ruin in my mind, and in my heart. After those three short months, I came home crazier than I had ever been in my entire life. My dad was worried and continued to ask me what happened to me out there. I couldn't share it with him or anyone else. I wanted to forget about it, yet it crept up on me day after day. Like a nightmare that I couldn't forget. I swore that I would never go back to that place.

During all that had happened to our family, my mom and my dad continued to serve God with all their hearts. In my opinion, they were given every reason to turn their backs on God. The enemy was having a feast with me as the downward spiral proved to go deeper than I had ever imagined. Both of my parents were attending a church in Stockton and my dad was helping. He still had not stepped back into the role as a pastor since he had been asked to step down. Yet he was just as involved in ministry to the capacity that he was able.

One of the pastors of the church in Stockton had a son who was a youth leader named Robbie. His secular job was a probation officer. I had known him for years and every time I found myself in juvenile hall, he would always reach out to me. He would talk to me, counsel me, and talk to me about change. Telling me that God has a plan for my life.

I still remember. It was a Wednesday night on Oct 21st, the year I had my teeth knocked out. In my heart, I was seeking the Lord in my life. I was planning to get together with some friends to celebrate one of their birthdays. Instead of going out, I felt compelled to go to the midweek service. I had been there a few times before that, but this time was different. I told my parents that I was going to church service with them. They were both getting ready to go, and they looked happily surprised. I didn't quite know what I was feeling, but the second I stepped into the church I couldn't stop the tears from falling down my face. I sat in the back, and throughout the service, I could not stop from sobbing. It was as if my soul was crying out to God in desperation. I truly believe that it was at this point that God began working on my heart. I never stopped believing in God, but I wanted to live my own life in my own way. I wanted to gang bang, party, and drink. The magnetic pull of God was getting stronger in my life. Yet, despite that important day, I continued in my path of darkness.

In the past, my father had given me a few cars. Something would always go bad and I'd ruin the opportunity. There was a time that for a few months I was working steadily and keeping my head straight. I was still out clubbing but I wasn't out of control. In comparison to my past, I had slowed my life down and was blessed by my dad with a Jaguar.

One of my cousins continued in the fast life and was now selling guns. He approached me one day and said, "Hey *primo*, I need to sell these guns tomorrow in Sacramento. Can I stash them in your car until tomorrow?"

I said, "Sure, just put them in my trunk." I didn't think much about it. I figured it wasn't a big deal and I wasn't planning on driving it. The next day I went to work, and my dad was working on one of his cars. He needed a jack and remembered that there was one in my trunk. Being that he gave the car to me he still had an extra set of keys. He walked over to my car and opened the trunk. There were two AK-47's and two bulletproof vests sitting in plain view. When I got home from work, my dad kicked me and my cousin out of the house. Matter of fact, my dad kicked everyone out of the house except my young brother and little sister. He cleaned house on that day. The only other person he didn't kick out was my brother Marco who was already in prison. I had nowhere to go, so I made my way to another uncle of ours in Atwater, Ca which is almost one hour south of Manteca. I was very thankful and glad that my uncle opened his door to me, but he was a severe alcoholic. My cousin had to move to Los Angeles to his grandma's house. My dad had called the cops on me several times, but now finding these guns was the last straw.

During this time my dad was approached by his neighbor and asked him if he needed a job. My dad explained to his neighbor that he had no experience. All he had ever done was pastoring and worked at canneries. So, after so many years in ministry, my dad stepped into the workforce and began employment at a bus factory in Hayward, Ca which is in the Bay Area. The drive was roughly ninety minutes west during commute hours. Very often the ninety-minute ride stretched to a slow crawl through the Altamont Hills that separated the Central Valley from the Bay Area. This was the norm for thousands of people that lived in the valley yet commuted to the Bay. It was always better pay and better jobs in the big cities of San Francisco, San Jose, Oakland, and other surrounding cities. The job, in combination with the long commute, became my dad's daily regimen, yet he never missed the mid-week Wednesday service or Sunday service. Work was a huge challenge for my dad, being that he hadn't worked outside of ministry for many years. His job consisted of building suspensions for the buses with many different types of people. Some were from a well-known motorcycle club. There was heavy metal music blaring all day long and my dad hated the job. Yet he knew he had to provide for his family. Even with a busy work life, serving God and going forward in the things of the Lord was always his priority.

One day in a meeting with some pastors, he began a conversation with pastor Jose, the man that led him to the Lord back in 1984. Pastor Jose was going to Colombia with a group of pastors to a leadership convention and invited my dad and mom to go with them. My dad wasn't really interested. He had a job and was feeling discouraged in the things of the Lord. He had given his entire life to the Lord, yet his family was completely shattered.

A few days later he was at work, once again the heavy metal was blaring out of the speakers and my dad was working on a suspension for a bus. Being at work trying to drown out the noise often led my dad to think about his life. It felt so long ago that God had spoken to him, almost as if the anointing of God had left. So many problems and situations led him to what he felt was a dry season in the spiritual sense. Then out of nowhere, my dad saw the vision again, the one the Lord showed him of me when I was five. It was the vision of me in Colombia yelling out, "*Colombia para Cristo.*" I believe my dad had lost hope for me by this point. Ever since my dad had kicked me out, I was so angry at him that we hadn't talked in over eight months. It was like giving a dying man CPR and breathing life into him once again. He whispered out, "Lord, you are still with me!"

At this point, I was now twenty-two years old and out running wild in Atwater. That same evening my dad called me. When my phone rang, my dad's voice was the last thing I expected to hear on the other end.

"Son, I want to talk to you," he said.

I knew that if my dad called me after not speaking to me for so long, that it must be serious. I drove up to his house without having the faintest idea of what he wanted. The second I walked into the house, my father began to excitably share with me all that had happened at work, with God showing him the vision. I had always respected my dad, even if I was angry with him for kicking me out. I would always hear him out when he would speak to me about God. When it came to the vision, the one he had of me in Colombia. Personally, I didn't believe it, yet I kept my composure as he spoke.

My dad continued, "There is a leadership conference in Colombia and your mom and I want you to go with us. If you pay for your ticket, we will take care of the rest."

I was confused and yet intrigued. Why would I go to a leadership conference with a bunch of pastors for two whole weeks? I was living my life exactly how I wanted to live it. I was working, clubbing and having a great time. I didn't know how to answer my dad, so I told him that I would go home and think about it. I thought back of that time when I was just a child and my dad sharing with me about the vision the Lord had given to him. Time after time over the years, even throughout my craziness, he would tell me that someday that vision would come true. After he would tell me about the vision, he would say that I would never be the same again.

I had to admit to myself that I truly was tired of the way I was living. I wanted a new life. I did want to change but I just couldn't do it. Matter of fact I had no idea how to live a normal life. Maybe my dad was right, maybe this was the plan of God all along. Maybe everything my dad said to me was true and it was my destiny and plan to go to Colombia with him. I found myself talking to God.

"God, this is my last time trying to change. I will go with my dad to Colombia. But if you don't change me, then it's over, and I will never change. God, I want this to be true."

I was desperate for a true change. I made up my mind that I would go. I had to see if this was God's plan for me. The very next day I put my car up for sale and sold it for five hundred dollars. I put in my two-week notice for vacation and purchased my passport. This was it, I was 100% committed. I would find out once and for all if everything my dad had been saying over the years was truly God's will.

The day finally came to meet my dad at his house at four o'clock in the morning. I knew I was going to be around a whole bunch of Christians, so I made sure to party the night before. I had to get it all out of my system. I knew what the next two weeks were going to be like. The hours passed by so quickly that I didn't get a chance to get any sleep. I was dropped off at my parent's house and when my dad saw me, his head just dropped. I didn't say a word to him. I just threw my bag into the trunk and just let myself drop into the backseat. My dad was disgusted at me and beyond upset. To this day I am still surprised that he still took me. There we were, my mom, my dad and myself on the way to the airport. Next stop, South America Colombia.

THE PLANE RIDE TO COLOMBIA

As we arrived at SFO (San Francisco International Airport), I felt like vomiting. There I was, trying to walk completely reeking as if I was doused in liquor. I was wearing an Oakland Raiders jersey, Raider sweat pants, with a NorCal beanie on my head. I looked like the stereotypical California thug. What contrasted the entire scene was my dad standing next to me in a complete suit and tie. As we walked into the terminal, I saw an entire group of about fifteen people waiting for us. The only one I recognized was pastor Jose, the man that led my dad to the Lord. Every single one of them was dressed as if they were going to a church service. I stood out so bad, and from the looks of my parents, I knew they were embarrassed. Each of these people were pastors and leaders of churches. I felt as if they were looking at me with the thought, 'what the heck is this guy doing here? Is he lost?' I had never felt so out of place in my entire life. What could I say, I was a bad pastor's son. They were all wide awake, happy and smiling with the excitement of going to the conference. I just needed to get to a seat before I passed out. As soon as I got my seat on the airplane, I slept most of the sixteen-hour flight. Before I knew it, we were landing in Bogota Colombia in South America. As I looked out of the window, I began to feel the excitement. This was the furthest I had ever been from California; the landscape was amazing. After the long flight and some much-needed sleep, I felt a lot better. I had paid five hundred dollars for the trip and was curious to see what was ahead. The entire city looked as if it was made of brick buildings. Someone had said that it was bigger than Los Angeles and by the looks of it, I believed it.

As soon as the plane stopped, everyone began getting their bags from the overhead bins that are above each passenger. I didn't quite know how to feel. Excited, nervous or happy? There I am, bag in hand, with a NorCal beanie on my head. I stepped down from the plane. I am not exaggerating, but the very second I stepped on Colombian soil, I distinctly heard, within my own heart and mind the words, 'You are going to stay here.' I stopped for a second and just stood still. I thought to myself, 'Am I still drunk, or am I going crazy? For sure I'm trippin.'

Once the entire group was together, we all gathered on a bus that was going to take us to our hotel. I was still feeling outside of myself. I quietly stepped onto the bus and was given a window seat. That voice within me wouldn't stop, 'You are going to stay here.' We began to drive through the city and I noticed almost every building was built in brick. I couldn't shake the feeling, like as if I was in another dimension. I don't know how to put into words what I was feeling. The city was so vast and full of people, yet it looked nothing like our cities in California. From the airplane window, the city looked like neat rows of nice brick buildings. Now actually going through the streets, I could see poverty, old homes, and a sense of danger. Coming from a thug background, I could feel the vibe of nothing good.

I thought to myself, 'What is the Lord up to?' Never in my wildest dreams did I ever think I would be on a bus going through the city of Bogota in the country of Colombia. Neither I or my family were of Colombian descent, and neither was the pastor that invited my dad to the conference. Could it really be true what my dad had told me all those years? Was my coming here really my destiny? I saw my entire life flash before me on that bus ride. The fights, the jail cells, the gangs, the drugs, my uncle when I was a young man, and the first time he offered me cocaine. I thought of the parties and the clubs in San Francisco, drunk and high and coming home without remembering how I got there. Also, the trip to Alaska and the things that happened there that completely changed me. I thought, 'God let this all be real... I am so tired of who I am.'

The next day the conference began. It was a well-known international event that happened once a year. Pastors and leaders from all around the world would come and be poured into, trained, and discipled for two entire weeks. It was a convention modeled after Jesus and the twelve disciples. Where each person would disciple twelve, and each of those twelve would disciple twelve more people. This was taught and was very effective when these pastors and leaders would go back to their local churches. They had internationally known speakers on their roster and I was looking forward to it. Once again there I was in the lobby of this huge facility, feeling like the oddball. It seemed like every man was wearing a suit, the women were unbelievably beautiful in nice colored dresses, yet there I was dressed like a typical gangbanger. Everywhere I looked I saw crazy Christians smiling. I couldn't stop looking around. My dad signaled to me that the service was about to start. I looked around one more time, then walked into the double doors to the auditorium. The Conference was about to begin. I thought to myself, 'What the heck am I doing here in this city, at this convention with all of these preachers. God, surely you have a sense of humor.'

8

THE CONFERENCE

I was now in Colombia with a decision to make. Was I going to waste my time and not even try, or was I going to surrender whole-heartedly to see if God truly wanted me? Right from the beginning, I felt the presence of God. It was undeniable. By the second day I realized that if I was going to find God, it was going to be in this place. My heart of stone began to melt. I remember the worship team was singing, and the entire building had their arms raised and their voices loud. It sounded as if I was in heaven with the entire heavenly angels and saints worshiping. Before I realized it, for the very first time, I had my own arms raised. I felt years and years of oppression break away with a gesture, so simple yet life-changing. It was as if the walls satan himself built around me, began crumbling. Tears began to stream down my face. Then I felt as if my hands needed to be lifted higher, it felt like I needed to clap louder. The Holy Spirit was like a giant magnet pulling me toward Him with an incredible force. When I closed my eyes, I could feel God standing directly in front of me. I had never felt anything remotely close to this in my entire life. Something was happening, and I had no idea what it was. This was a leadership conference, not an outreach to sinners. There were no altar calls for salvation or talk of repentance. The sermons were directed at leaders. The training and teachings were directed at leadership. Yet, it was during worship that God was using this leadership conference to reach me, the worst sinner that I knew. When I first arrived, I heard a voice within say, 'You are going to stay here'. By the fourth day, it wasn't so much a voice but a tug within my brain and heart, and the tug was relentless. It wouldn't leave me alone.

The tug became so unbearable that I approached my dad. I needed to talk to him. He was completely astonished by the fourth day, as he watched the Lord deal with me. I knew my mom and dad were seeing a miracle before their eyes. They never bothered to say anything to me, they were just standing back and allowing the Lord to move in my heart. So, there we were in the hotel lobby, watching the NFL Super Bowl with the Raiders and the Buccaneers. We were both together, I was excited about the game. My dad knew that I was a Raider fan. It was there that I couldn't hold it any longer and began to share my heart with my dad.

"Look pops, I want to talk to you about something."

My dad and I have a very close relationship when things are good between us.

I continued, "Something inside of me is telling me to stay here in Colombia. I don't know what's going on, but I know it's the will of God."

He just looked at me and said, "Let's pray mijo. If this is God's will, He will open the door for it to happen." We prayed together and left it at that.

Each church that was visiting the conference was assigned a local guide. The organization of the entire conference was top notch, and this extended to the guide also. That way we wouldn't get lost or end up in an unsafe area in the vast city of Bogota. Our guide was named Daniel. He would take us back and forth from our hotel and the conference, also taking us sightseeing and shopping. He was in his early twenties like me and was attending the university. By the sixth day, our group of fifteen was having a wonderful Colombian breakfast. Everyone was talking and ecstatic about what they were learning at the conference.

Daniel, the guide, stood up and said he had an announcement. "I would like to thank you all for coming and participating in our annual conference. I would like to share with you that we have an eighteen-month program for leaders at the leadership school here in Bogota. We will fully train and prepare you for leadership wherever you go. It can be arranged for anyone of you to stay and get plugged into the Leadership school."

My heart began to pound. I knew this was it. This is exactly why I am here in Colombia. This is why my dad was given that vision so many years ago. I leaned over to my dad and whispered, "That's for me dad! he is talking about me." I knew without a shadow of a doubt that this announcement was specifically for me. My dad just looked at me. To this day I don't know what went through his head. We were so far away from home and I was a baby in the Lord. I had surrendered to Christ just a few short days before, now I was willing to lay all my cards on the table for the Lord. To this very day, I know it was the will of God that I stay. The conference was for two weeks. I had a job waiting for me, a life waiting for me, and a return flight ticket. I was about to lose it all, and I didn't care.

I sat down with my parents and Daniel to talk with them about staying. I shared my heart with them of the things I was feeling. They listened with open hearts and all agreed that I should stay to follow the will of God. We made the arrangements for my room and board, and the admission into the Leadership school. I was introduced to Daniel's parents and they said I could stay with them once the conference was over. They were a very welcoming classy family. I even want to note something I feel a need to say. Daniel and his family are the best examples of what a family should be like that I had ever had the privilege of meeting. They especially taught me how people should treat each other. I was able to see the class of the Colombian people through them. They were simply awesome. The mother was a dentist and the father had also been involved in politics in the city. He was the treasurer for the big church in Bogota where the conference was being held. Yet they were still ready to accept a California thug like me. I was overwhelmed with gratitude.

I walked away from the conversation with my mind in overdrive. Colombia was not just a few hundred miles away, it was nations away. I still had a little bit of money from working and from selling my car. I thank God that my parents were willing to also financially support my stay. I was only twenty-two years old and somewhat afraid of the unknown. Yet there was an excitement in my heart that I had never felt. I thought, 'God, what are you going to do in my life?'

The day finally came for my parents to leave back to the United States. They packed their bags and we all just looked at each other. The Hotel was still booked until the following morning, so I was going to stay there until later that night. Daniel had arranged to pick me up later that night to take me to his house. I stood with my parents at the door of the hotel room. We were happy, afraid and amazed all at the same time. So much had happened in the two short weeks we were there. I arrived hung over from a night of partying and drinking, and now here I was. Sober-minded and ready to release myself into the complete will of God. The second they walked down the hallway, and the door of the hotel room closed, it truly hit me. They were gone, my plane ticket is gone, and my life back home is gone. The reality that I was really going to do this. I remember thinking, 'this is crazy.' Yet, I had peace in my heart. The tug in my heart to stay was solid, but I didn't truly know what that meant. Was I staying for the eighteen months of leadership school? Was I going to stay for the rest of my life? I had no idea. I was anxious to see the place where I was going to stay. Up to this point, I still had no idea where I was going to live, much less know where Daniel lived. All I knew was that the place where I was staying was in the outskirts of Bogota called Cajica. Now as I look back, I realize that I was a bit crazy and brave. In serving God I have learned that we will never be in His will, unless there is a bit of craziness and bravery every step of the way. God flourishes in our lives when we are ripped out of our comfort zone and into the unknown. How can our steps be guided and ordered by the Lord if we already know the steps ahead of us? That is what is wrong with modern Christianity, we want to package Christianity like a vacation itinerary. A sort of scheduled moment by moment checklist that we approve of before buying into it.

I had to wait for my ride with Daniel. He was a student at the university and would attend from morning until the evening. I waited hours for Daniel to pick me up. For some reason, the minutes passed so slow as I sat in the room alone. Finally, Daniel knocked on the door. I was so happy to see him. I quickly grabbed my bags and quickly checked out of the room. We took a bus ride to the outskirts of Cajica. I still had no idea where I was going to stay, other than Daniel's parents' house. When we finally arrive, he walks me to the back of the house and shows me a small backroom.

He says, "This is where you'll be sleeping."

I thought to myself, 'oh wow... here?' I was very grateful to him and his family, but this was not a bedroom. The only thing I can compare it to is a washroom in the back of older homes in the United States. My heart sank as I looked around. There was no bed, no blankets, no furniture, nothing. 'This is where I will be staying for the next year and a half? Okay Lord, let Your will be done.'

I saw God move in my life right away. Within a minute, someone came and told me that they had a bed available for me. I quickly made my way to the house of the person offering the bed and a blanket. And within an hour I was in my own apartment. To this day I still don't know how this all happened. There was absolutely no furniture in the entire apartment except my bed and my blanket. The apartment was the nicest place in the entire neighborhood and even rivaled a nice apartment back in the states. It was gorgeous with a fireplace and a high-class architecture. I was completely in shock as I sat on my bed in my own place. Just a few hours ago I was willing to sleep in a small backroom with no bed, and some way, somehow, the Lord opened doors and provided. Daniel lived only four blocks away which was also going to be a huge help because he was the only living soul that I considered a friend in this far away country.

The very first thing I did in my first week, was going with Daniel to the school to enroll. It was not at the main sanctuary where the conference was held. It was a huge church with many campuses and buildings in different locations throughout the city. What made it easier was the fact that I am fluent in Spanish, so the transition wasn't much of a problem. The classes and homework were all written and taught in Spanish. The only hiccup I did have was the fact that I didn't know how to write in Spanish.

They made exceptions and allowed me to turn in my homework in English.

I had never lived in a big city before so there was so much to get acclimated to. The school was thirty minutes away from my apartment which was in Cajica, and the school was in Bogota. I had to learn the bus system, so I could be mobile to get from place to place. Not just the school but for other necessities. I knew that Daniel wasn't always going to be available. In the first few days, I went with Daniel, as he showed me how the system worked. Within a few days, I would take bus trips all over the city to sight-see and really get a feel for this old beautiful city. I found out where the malls were at and I'd spend the day walking around. I also found out which bus to take to get to the theater that would show American movies with Spanish subtitles. I did all these things alone.

Back home I lost my job. My mom worked at the same place where I was employed, and she told my manager that I wasn't coming back. Girls I would hang out with and go out with never heard from me. I never bothered to contact them. I completely dropped off the face of the earth from everything I left behind in California.

Each Sunday I attended service at the megachurch that was filled by thousands of people. When I say it was a mega church, I don't mean in the way an American would define a mega church. This was more of a coliseum with sections, much the same way our sports coliseums are built. Each leader would sit in assigned sections with the people they would bring. It was completely organized. After a few weeks, I volunteered as an usher for the section I belonged to. I remember at one point the pastor mentioned that there were two Americans amongst them. They had come all the way from America to learn what they teach here in the school of Leadership of Colombia. The pastor was motivating the Colombians by letting them know that even foreigners came to learn. I was excited because I knew they were talking about me and another brother named John. John was from Texas and had a job teaching English to the locals. He even offered to help me in getting a job teaching English to the Spanish speakers. I declined because I didn't come to Colombia to work, I came to learn. I will never forget this time in my life. For the first time, I felt real peace in my heart. I know that it was Christ giving me that peace, but I'm forever indebted to Bogota Colombia for being the vessel that God used to draw me closer to Him.

9

36 CHAIRS

Once I was settled in, enrolled and knew my way around some of the city, things were going along smoothly. I was becoming someone that I never imagined I could be. I had so much self-control, which was something I never had in all the years of my life. There were so many beautiful women that were after me in the city of Bogota and Cajica. The queen of Cajica would come to the church to see me, yet for the first time, I had no desire for those things. I had no desire for the party life, alcohol or marijuana. My mindset was the complete opposite of where I was in California. I loved what I was learning, and I truly enjoyed volunteering at the church and attending there. I was meeting very inspiring influential people. It was to the point that I never wanted to go back to the United States. This is exactly what I needed. Back home there was nothing but destruction, heartache, and pain. I was done with the United States. I could just furnish my apartment and begin a new life here as a Colombian. I was going to get plugged in deeper at the church and become a leader. I was ready to completely let go and do whatever it was that God wanted in my life. I would call home to my parents once a week to share with them how my life was going. We finally had great communication with each other. Yet, little did I know that God had his own plans.

Daily prayer was key and highly emphasized in my training. We were shown in the bible where it said in the book of Psalm chapter five verse three.

O LORD, in the morning you hear my voice; in the morning I prepare a sacrifice for you and watch.

Each day I would get up early before the sun was up so I could pray. I would put on my alarm at three thirty in the morning, get myself ready, and go into prayer until I had no prayer in me. Then after that, I would go back to sleep.

One day I was in prayer in my room and God taught me how he wanted me to pray. He wanted me to write down a prayer hit list. The Lord would put people on my heart to add to that list. It was very similar in the way the gangs of the world use a hit list for people they want to destroy. Yet my hit list wouldn't destroy, it would bring life. In the carnal world, being on a hit list was not good at all. It would bring terror to a person because it meant that you were green-lighted to be executed. A green light meant that it was a 'go' for anyone that came across you. They wouldn't need permission or excuse, it was kill on sight. This was molded into anyone that grew up in the gang street life. I began to pray and write down names, then after looking at my piece of paper, I realized it was a hit list. God has a hit list for people. This was my hit list, a list of people to pray for. Some for salvation, some for healing, some for the trouble they were having in their life. I had a hit for my own friends. For their salvation, for their addictions, for their alcoholism. I even had my enemies on that piece of paper. For the first time in my life, I was praying for enemies. As the days passed, God would put more people in my mind. The list continued to grow. Each morning I would open my list and go to war in the Spirit for each of these people. God was using the mold that I had been taught in the world and was using it for His Glory. I would pray for hours for these people and from that day on I called it my prayer hit list.

One day I woke up on my regular schedule. I would read the bible then get right into prayer. There was nothing different as I went through my prayer hit list. By this time, I was also working on my school projects every day. Once I finished my school work, I went to take a shower. I had some errands to do that day. While showering I heard that clear voice once again, speak to my soul. The same voice that said I was going to stay in Colombia. The voice said,' buy thirty-six chairs.' It was as if the voice was echoing. 'Buy thirty-six chairs, buy thirty-six chairs, buy thirty-six chairs,' I knew it was God. There was no doubt in my mind. I didn't hesitate, doubt, or ignore it. I simply accepted it in my heart. I quickly asked Daniel if he and his dad could take me to a store, so I could buy them. They both agreed to take me, and I bought all the thirty-six lawn chairs. The type of chairs you would put in your backyard or in your front porch. Even though they both took me and helped me, I could see on their faces that they weren't sure what to think. I couldn't stop talking about the voice of God. I was so excited because I knew that the Lord must have a huge plan for these thirty-six chairs. I brought them back to my empty apartment and I set them up in the living room in rows.

All my life I had seen my dad plant churches in buildings, houses, and garages. I have helped him so many times by setting up chairs and knocking down walls. I never bothered to understand what the drive was in my dad as I was growing up, but by seeing him as my example, it has helped me to see the outcome. Many times, if we are short-sighted, we fail to truly see what God is doing. Instead, we get filled with doubt and the things of God in our lives are aborted before given a chance to live. As I sat back and saw the chairs lined up, I figured that it would be a place for bible study or prayer. Never in my wildest dreams did I know it would become what it became. To think that my plans were to furnish the living room with some couches or maybe some end tables with lamps. God's ways are not our ways and our thoughts are not God's thoughts.

It was during this time that I asked Daniel to come to live with me in the two-bedroom apartment. He agreed, even though he was hardly there. Schooling was very important to him and he was gone every single day until late at night. One day we were both sitting there staring at the thirty-six chairs and I began to share my heart with Daniel.

I said, "Look, brother, I'll evangelize every day while you are at the university. You know the bible so much more than me, so you can share the Word. I'll invite every single person

I come across and we can gather here and talk about God. Let's see how we do."

I don't know for a fact if this was the first Christian gathering in the town of Cajica. What I did know is that every day I traveled around the town of Cajica and I never saw a Christian church in existence. Every day I talked with people and no Christian gathering was ever mentioned. I had to travel all the way to Bogota for service or bible study.

Daniel heard me out about what I proposed and said, "Okay brother Alfonso, let's pray for two weeks for direction and wisdom from God on how we should do it."

I agreed and began right away. Every single morning, we would wake up and pray for the entire apartment and I would lay hands on each chair one by one, every single day.'

"Lord, I know that you spoke to me about purchasing these chairs. I pray for each chair, and in doing that, I am praying that you send someone to sit on this chair. As they sit here, that you will move in their hearts. That you bring salvation and healing to them. That you move powerfully in their lives that will leave no shadow of a doubt that you are God, and that you love them. I pray for your anointing on every square inch of this apartment. That this apartment be dedicated for you and for your works. That this place is holy ground for all that step in. I pray for your angels to encircle this place in protection against the enemy and against the plans of the enemy. I pray for hearts to be broken into pieces and that you give them a new heart and a new Spirit. For your Spirit to dwell in them. In Jesus mighty and powerful name, amen."

Since Daniel was always in school, he couldn't help me evangelize. This worked out perfect because I wasn't a public speaker, but I was good at talking to strangers on the street. Once they would show up, Daniel would be the one speaking and giving a bible study. He did have two sisters that were willing to help me, as well as a few people from the Bogota church that lived in Cajica. One of Daniel's sisters was a computer engineer and was able to design a nice flier. With those fliers we began to comb through the streets, stores, and neighborhood, inviting them to come fellowship each Wednesday evening. One day our small group went up to the mountain that overlooks Cajica and we all prayed for the entire city and its occupants. I was so excited, as the days came closer to our first Wednesday meeting. We had prayed for two weeks and evangelized to every person we came across.

Then the day finally came. It was getting close to the time that was posted on the fliers, at seven o'clock. I was nervous, not sure how to feel. I had so many questions in my heart. Was anyone going to show up? Did we pass out enough fliers? Were they even interested in Jesus? Then it was time and people began to show up. They walked up the steps and walked in. I was so happy. Attendance was between ten to fifteen people. Some of them were from the church, some were local neighbors and some I had never seen before.

Once everyone was settled in, we started off with prayer. Then Daniel stepped up and began giving a lesson that we had learned in the Bogota church. I did not speak, nor did I expect to. I knew I had already done what God willed me to do. To buy the thirty-six chairs and to evangelize and invite. One plants, and one waters, but only God brings the growth. By the end of the meeting, I had a huge smile, not only on my face but on my heart.

When the second week came around, the attendance jumped to fifty people. This was with no evangelism or fliers anymore. Every single chair was full and there were many that were standing up along the walls. There were people on the balcony that couldn't fit inside. The first week I was happy, but now I was in complete shock. By this time, I knew that something was happening. As I looked around, I didn't recognize them. I knew that I hadn't invited them. By the third week, I stood in the back looking at everyone. Daniel was up front preaching and there were so many people, that many of them had to stand outside. The chairs were full, the walls were lined with people standing up, the balcony was full, and people were outside trying to get in to hear the gospel. I thought to myself, 'God is doing something tremendous right now.' I could see the fingerprints of God everywhere. I had offered coffee and bread for everyone. People were having a good time as they came to hear about Jesus.

After that third week, Daniel's dad went to the church in Bogota to tell them of what God was doing. His dad was the treasurer of the megachurch and knew all the leadership there. One day I was picked up in a car and taken to a meeting. I didn't even know that a meeting was in place until I arrived. I was only twenty-two years old and I had no idea where they were taking me. Next thing I know we pull up to the megachurch and I'm taken into an office with a very professional looking man sitting there.

I sat down, and he began to explain to me, "We have been trying to open a church in Cajica for the last ten years. We have not been able to do it."

After he finished explaining the situation to me and the dire need of a church in Cajica.

I replied back, "Sir, this is not my church or something of mine. What is happening belongs to God. If you feel that you can send leadership there, let God's will be done."

Right away they brought in one of their top leaders, Jorge Rojas to pastor the church that was taking place in my apartment. Daniel had no problem with it because Jorge was Daniel's leader. They prayed for me and spoke a Word into my life.

They knew about my dad and said, "Your Dad is like King David and you are like Solomon his son. All the seeds of your father's ministry are going to be seen in your life. Your brother that is not with you, God has him in the palm of His hand."

At that time my brother was in prison and I knew they were talking about him. My knees buckled, and I fell to the ground. So many words of knowledge were spoken into my life during those few weeks.

By the fourth meeting, Jorge Rojas showed up to my apartment and we spoke for the first time. He brought with him a worship leader and equipment also. I wasn't ready to pastor a church, I didn't know what I was doing. All I knew was that God told me to buy thirty-six chairs. It was a relief when a man of God like Jorge showed up to lead. It was a huge blessing. In a matter of weeks, my apartment was now the beacon of light for Jesus in the town of Cajica. Within a month of meeting there with Jorge Rojas as the pastor, we had to move to a bigger warehouse that was two blocks away from the apartment. By this time, it was out of my hands and within weeks the warehouse wasn't big enough to hold the people that were hungry to hear the Word of God.

By this time so much had happened in such a short time. I was staying in Colombia, I was plugged into the leadership school, God told me to buy thirty-six chairs, and now out of my apartment, a church was birthed in Cajica. One of the first Christian churches. I felt like I was on complete fire for the Lord. I was now five months into my stay in Colombia. Each month I had to travel to the local immigration office to get stamped, but after six months I had to leave Colombia, or I would be considered an illegal visitor. Daniel's dad would take me, and they would always want to know where I was staying at and other basic information. After my fifth stamp, the reality hit me that I would have to leave soon. I thought to myself, 'what is going to happen?' My schooling was an eighteen-month curriculum. I still had the apartment, which I never furnished. The church had moved into a bigger building along with the chairs I purchased. My dad had an idea of having me leave to nearby Ecuador for two days then coming back to Colombia to start another six months stay.

There was nothing more I could do except to pray for direction. One day I woke up to my regular daily routine and went down the list of names in prayer. Once I finished my morning prayers I walked back to my room, laid down and instantly fell asleep. Suddenly, I was taken from my sleep state to a place I had never been to. God was about to reveal to me a powerful vision. This had never happened before in my life. Yes, I've heard His voice and I've felt His presence. But nothing like this had ever happened to me. I was about to step into another spiritual realm.

10

BLOODY RED DIRT

I had two more weeks to go before I had to leave Colombia. I was praying every day for direction on what to do. Then one day I was given a vision. I was in a deep sleep where I found myself in a strange place. I was walking on a dirt road not sure where I was heading to. I looked to the right and I saw nothing but dirt for miles. I noticed that all the dirt looked blood red. It was a very high contrasting color of red. Even in the dream, I knew that it wasn't a normal color for dirt. I continued to walk and looked to my left side. I saw huts built by indigenous people. They were selling beads and homemade clothes. I began to look at all the huts with merchandise and yet I didn't stop walking. I was being pulled to walk forward. I wasn't sure if it was a city or village. To the right, it continued to be miles of dirt and to the left an endless number of huts. I reached a point where I could have continued to walk straight, turn right or turn left. I decided to turn left. The huts continued to fill the areas around the dirt road. I continued to walk and came upon a giant white tent. It was enormous, very much like a carnival or circus tent. It was so big that I estimate it could have fit five thousand people. As soon as I saw the tent, I felt the power of God in a way that it shook and jolted everything in me. I had never felt His presence so intensely. I wondered, 'what is going on in that building? Is there a fire inside?' I continued to walk toward it. When I finally reached the entrance, I didn't know what to expect. I slowly walked in and looked around. There was no fire, it was practically empty. There were rows and rows of empty chairs. Finally, I saw five or six people, some sitting, some standing. They were worshiping God with all their hearts. I felt confused because the power of God was so intense, yet the tent was empty besides the handful of people that were worshiping. Then I noticed that someone was preaching at the pulpit. I looked up and saw a white man walking back and forth on the stage and he was praying or worshiping, I couldn't tell. Then I noticed that he had two black assistants sitting down. 'What is going on?' I thought to myself.

The white man behind the pulpit stopped what he was doing and looked right at me. He walked straight to me and took me to a different room. This room was made with panels of wood that allowed light from outside to come in between the beams.

He was now sitting and said, "You are going to come to Brazil! You are going to come to Brazil. You need to come to Brazil."

At that point, I woke up and I had to shake myself awake. I laid there trying to remember and grasp all that I saw. I didn't understand any of it. Once I realized that I was now awake, I quickly jumped out of my bed and walked over to Daniel's room. I was knocking so hard It must have sounded like I was going to break down the door.

"Daniel! Daniel! Open the door... I just had a vision!" He opened the door and I just explained to him everything I saw. I couldn't keep up with my own words, I was so excited. Once I finished describing all that I saw, I waited to see what Daniel would say.

"Brother, I believe that God is going to take you to Brazil one day," said Daniel. We immediately prayed together and that was the end of it. I decided that I would not share this vision until it was time. I never mentioned it to my dad, to the leaders in the church, nobody. I would hold it close to my heart. If this was God's will for me, I wanted to see it unfold in God's time. I might not have understood the entire dream, but one thing I did know, I knew that I would go to Brazil one day. I just didn't know how soon.

The next day I called my dad to see how he was doing back in California. Up until this time, he was still working in the bay area. What I didn't expect was the good news that my dad shared. He was going to go back into full-time ministry by pastoring a church in Modesto Ca. Once he told me the good news, he explained how it all went down.

My dad was asleep and had a vision of a pastor that was dying. In the vision, my dad grabbed the pastor's hand to comfort him.

Then the dying man said, "Come to pastor my church. You need to pastor this church."

Soon after that a Baptist church called my dad and asked

him to come to speak. The church was looking for a pastor because their pastor had passed away. My dad was not from a Baptist background, nor was he credentialed by the Baptist church. On his first time speaking there, he told the congregation.

"God has called me to pastor this church." Within weeks he was chosen to be the senior pastor of *Rosa de Saron* Baptist church.

When my dad shared his vision and the story of how it all went down, I was so excited for my dad. For so long he had not pastored, and I knew it was in his heart. All my dad wanted to do was serve God. To do it full time was a huge blessing for him. By this time, it had been seven or eight years since my dad was in full-time ministry.

"I'm so excited for you dad!" I said. I knew that God was doing something amazing in the life of our family. My dad immediately gave up his $33 dollar an hour job to go pastor a church for $12 an hour without hesitation.

After the phone call with my dad, I sat down with Daniel. We were playing dominoes. I had taught him how to play the way we did in California.

I said, "Daniel... I feel in my heart that my time is done here in Colombia. God has done great things in Cajica, and in my life. My dad is going to start pastoring again, brother, I think I should be with him to help him. My time is done."

As we spoke, I reflected of my first time stepping into Colombia still hung over from partying the night before. I thought of the conference and of the voice of God telling me to buy thirty-six chairs. My apartment full of people, and pastor Jorge coming to preach. Cajica having a place of worship, after ten years of trying by the church in Bogota. Daniel listened to me and he agreed. I didn't want to go to Ecuador just to come back. I needed to go home.

It was my last week in Colombia and Daniel took me to the best place to purchase a suit in all of Colombia, it was called *Arturo Calle*. I was so excited as I tried on a suit. I felt like a million bucks, I had never worn a suit in my life. I wanted to go home with that appearance, I wanted my outside to show how I felt inside. I arrived in Colombia in a football jersey, and I wanted to go home in a suit. I felt like my mom and dad deserved to see me like that. I was a new man. All because of my dad inviting me with him to the conference. I simply wanted to bless my parents. When I was living reckless, I would have killed for my dad. I would have done anything for him in my own ignorant way. I always respected them both and loved them both, but I just never knew how to live my life correctly.

I was able to say goodbye to pastor Jorge Rojas, to the leaders that embraced me. I cried many tears with them as the day of leaving counted down. I was able to thank Daniel and his family. It was like a part of me didn't want to leave, yet I knew I had to leave. At one time I thought I would never leave Colombia for the rest of my life. Yet, I knew that God had more plans for me. I just had to follow where ever He was leading. Maybe God wanted me to use the leadership skills I had learned to help my dad at the new church. I was even asked by the church leaders in Bogota to be a part of the international team to help bring up leaders for the Bogota church in California. I didn't know what was ahead of me, but one thing I did know. God was with me. I said my last goodbyes at the airport and boarded the plane. I was on my way home. Back to the United States.

11

COMING HOME

My plane began a slow descent that broke through the clouds into the San Francisco Bay area. I felt excited to be home and to see my family. I knew that my mom and dad were waiting for me as I landed. When they saw me walk up to them in a suit, they were shocked at the transformation. We cried tears of joy as we embraced each other. I hugged my mom for a very long time as we cried together, my dad stood back in awe. It was a very happy time for us. Once again, I couldn't help but think of the contrast since the day I left in this same airport. I was drunk and my father was rightfully ashamed of me. Yet now, I saw pride in his eyes toward me. It felt so good.

We had so many things to talk about. I wanted to pour everything out of my experience in Colombia, and my dad wanted to pour out everything that was happening with the new church in Modesto. We kept stumbling over each other's words. We walked to the car and we all continued talking as I sat in the back seat. I continued to talk about my experience, my dad continued to talk about the church.

In the middle of that, my mom continued to talk about how nice I looked in a suit. It was like three different conversations all happening at once all the way home.

During this period my parents decided to allow me to come back home, which was a big blessing that I didn't expect. I had earned my dads trust back, it meant the world to me. Also, by being gone for so long, I had no job, no finances, and no car. Being at my parent's house was going to help me to get back on my feet. It felt as if I had to restart my life and recondition myself to live in California once again.

A few days before I left Colombia, I began to feel a slight pain in my back-wisdom teeth. By the time I was home, I needed immediate attention. My mom made an appointment for me the next day at Western Dental in Stockton. I had no money, so my mom paid $250 to have the tooth extracted. This was done on a Monday, but when Wednesday came around, I still wasn't feeling 100%. This was a letdown because by this time my dad had been pastoring at the church and was looking forward to me attending for the first time. I was also looking forward to attending the midweek service. I knew that there was a special speaker, which was always a treat. I had no idea who the speaker was or where he came from. All my mom and dad said was that it was going to be a very powerful night. I still hadn't seen the church or met any of the people. My dad had shared with them about my experience and many were waiting to hear my story. I decided I would stay home and rest. The timing wasn't right yet.

After a few hours, I was resting at the house and my mom called.

"Mijo, the visitor is going to be staying the night with us, is it okay if he uses your room? I know you just got home, and I know you don't feel well."

"It's okay mom."

I always had respect for a man of God. Especially where I was at in my heart and mind after experiencing all that I did in Colombia. I grew up with my dad always opening his home to visiting missionaries or evangelists. I didn't think much of it anymore, except for the fact that I was still feeling down and unable to attend.

My mom arrived first. She begins to put her purse and bible down all while talking. She was so excited and began sharing with me all that had happened at the church service.

My mom said, "You should have gone mijo! It was an amazing service. The testimonies and stories were so powerful... especially the missionary, the guest speaker from Brazil."

My heart stopped. Did she just say Brazil? My mind began whirling. I had never told anyone other than Daniel about my vision of the bloody red dirt, or the white man with two black assistants. I began to feel the presence of God. I didn't say anything more to my mom. I quickly walked outside to get some air. I didn't know what this meant, but I knew that this could very well tie into the vision the Lord gave me. I didn't want to do or say the wrong thing when this man came into the house.

As I walked, I began to pray for direction. I knew that I

can get excited and just jump into a conversation without thinking first. One thing I know about myself is that I'm high idled and have a massive drive in whatever direction I go, whether good or bad. Whatever it may be, I go full blast, guns blazing, and the gas pedal to the metal.

"God control me, please. Control my emotions and my tongue. I'm not sure what is going on. Did the vision have to do with this man? Please give me a confirmation in my heart."

I walked around my neighborhood and prayed. Seeking direction and wisdom for about a half hour before I decided to return home. I knew that by the time I would arrive home, my dad would be back with the man from Brazil and another pastor.

As I walked into the house, I saw pastor Enrique and missionary Pedrino. He was a simple looking man with glasses. He was not Mexican, he looked more Portuguese. I had never seen him before. He was sitting at the table with my mom and dad. They both stood up and introduced themselves to me as I also introduced myself. While I was out for a walk my parents began to share with them of my story of the last few months. I thank God that my parents had a good story to share about one of their children. Anytime before this, I'm sure my parents were embarrassed when asked about their grown children. I began to also share of the lifestyle I came out of as they both sat listening intently.

The missionary began to explain to me what he did. That he was the director of a missionary preparation school in

Brazil. It was called Ambassador school. They train missionaries to travel all around the world and serve the people for Jesus.

Then he said, "I hear of all the great things that happened in Colombia with you over the last few months."

Even though I was grateful for the things he was saying, I didn't want to talk about Colombia. I was driven to the fact that he was from Brazil. This was no coincidence. I had a vision from a man telling me I had to go to Brazil, and here in my kitchen, within days of returning was a missionary from Brazil. I felt led to finally share my vision with this man.

I said, "Yes, God did amazing things in Colombia. Things that I never imagined in my life. God started a church in my apartment and transformed my life. But I need to share with you of a vision I received from God a few days before I came home. I don't know if it's with you, or with someone else. But God has called me to come to Brazil."

I had no idea whether the vision was tied to this man or not, but I began to share everything that I saw. My parents didn't know what was going on, they had no idea of this vision. They knew that God did a work in my life, but now I was speaking about a vision. They never heard me speak like this before. I had just been home for three days and they hadn't seen me in six months. I think they were still feeling me out to see if this was all real. I had brought so many problems and destruction to myself and to my family, so I didn't blame them for wondering these things.

When I finished sharing my vision to the missionary, he

was looking at me with a blank stare, his mouth had dropped a bit and I believe he was speechless for a moment. This man had seen miracles all over the world, Africa, Europe. They both traveled the world. It was a moment of pure confirmation for me when he began to share with me.

The missionary began to speak. "The place where I am from in Paulinia, Brazil. It is well known and recognized because of how red the dirt is. In my school of Ambassador, the dirt is red, but I can see how someone can describe it as bloody red dirt."

It was like someone dropped a bomb on me. That was a 100% accurate complete confirmation of my vision. It was so intense, and I was totally pumped up. I knew that this meeting was the plan of God. My parents were looking back and forth from the missionary to me. They heard about my vision for the first time at this table and heard the confirmation about the dirt.

The missionary continued to speak. "The people from my village are very dark skinned. There is only one white man that came all the way from Europe years ago as a missionary... He came to my area in the Amazon and has stayed there. This man is my pastor, and he does have two black assistants."

I had no words to say, and I didn't even know what to think after all the missionary said. All I could think was, 'God, where do we go from here?' One thing I did know was I would be going to Brazil to see this man's pastor. Even from Colombia, I knew that I was going to be a missionary to preach Christ to the nations. I knew that nothing was going to stop me and nowhere was too far for me. After seeing what God did in Colombia and in my life, I knew that He could take me anywhere in the world. After we talked more, we all decided to pray together for direction and to thank God for all He was doing in our lives.

After the prayer, the missionary said, "You are going back to Brazil with me." As soon as he said that, the pastor that came with him began looking for flight tickets on the computer for me. Within a few minutes, they found all the information they needed, not only for the flight but for a temporary visa to travel. Within two days I was given clearance and I was boarding a plane to Brazil. To this day I have no idea who paid for that plane ticket, but I thank God for opening doors that nobody can shut. I hadn't been home a week yet from Colombia, and here I was, within days of coming back home, headed to Brazil. I did not even have a chance to visit my dad's church.

I had boarded the plane alone, flew to Florida to change flights. Then from there, I landed in Sao Paulo, Brazil. Thinking back, I still can't believe I did that. I was truly on a mission for God.

BRAZIL

I was now on a seventeen-hour flight. Once again, I would be landing in a foreign nation that I had never been to, much less thought I would ever be at. I looked out of the window as we dropped elevation into the airport in San Paulo, Brazil. The city was massive and is one of the most populated cities in the world with over twelve million people. As a reference point for anyone reading this book from the United States, Los Angeles has a population of four million people and New York is over eight million. As I walked off of the plane into the airport, I felt nervous. I had no guide waiting for me nor did I speak Portuguese, which made it challenging. At least in Colombia, I spoke fluent Spanish. The airport was milling with hundreds of people from all parts of the world. It was during soccer season, and Boca Junior, a professional team from Argentina was there in the terminal singing their national anthem. I learned very quickly how popular soccer is in South America. I knew it was going to be tricky getting around. I just began walking the direction I felt I needed to go to get out of the airport. Somehow, I needed to find the bus that would take me on a three-hour bus ride to the missionary preparation school. I had no idea how I was going to make this happen.

As I stood in the long line for customs, I remembered that my mom told me that pastor Enrique, the man that brought Missionary Pedrino to my house had a son. They were from Los Angeles and his son Israel was also going to attend the missionary preparation school. My mom told me this because he spoke English and I would have someone to talk to during my stay in Brazil. As I was thinking about these things, I noticed a young man nervously looking through his bags. By looking at the brands he was wearing I guessed that he was an American.

I decided to ask, "Hello, it looks like you lost something?" Sure enough, he answered me in English.

"Yeah, I can't find my information that I need. Customs won't let me into the country until I find the information from the school I will be going to." He said with a worried look on his face as he flipped through his bag over and over. Then he introduced himself.

"My name is Israel."

"You're Israel? I'm Alfonso!" I answered.

Come to find out, it was pastor Enrique's son, Israel. He had also heard about me from his father and even knew about my trip to Colombia. What he was looking for was his itinerary with all of the school information. Without that information, he would not have been able to proceed into the country. They needed to know exactly why you were there, what address were you staying at, and phone numbers for your destination. Since we had the same itinerary, we were both able to get through customs. This blessing was not just one-sided in helping him get through. Because once I arrived, I quickly realized that without a guide, I would have been completely lost. I actually believe that if Israel hadn't been there, there was no way I would have made it to the school. Thank God that Israel knew what bus to get on, and how to get on the right bus. We needed each other to get to the destination. This entire situation was a miracle on its own.

During the three-hour bus ride, I was able to share with him all of my experience in Colombia. We had a great time as we talked about our lives and what God was doing. We were both very excited about what was going to happen at the missionary preparation school. Finally, after riding for hours on the practically empty bus, we arrived at the school of Ambassadors in the city of Paulinia. The school's bible verse is so fitting on who they are.

2 Corinthians 5:20 *Now then, we are ambassadors for Christ, as though God were pleading through us: we implore you on Christ's behalf, be reconciled to God.*

The school curriculum was one month of intense training. The first two weeks in Bible training and prayer, then the second half we would spend deep in the Amazon jungle with the indigenous people of Brazil. We were in a class all day long for the first two weeks. At times we were sent out to walk around the school to pray, to get your heart, mind, and soul ready for the Amazon jungle. Other times we would open our Bibles and learn years worth of

Scripture in a matter of days. I had been in the church all my life because of my dad, but I never truly grasped any of it. Here in this small class setting, I was completely focused. There was no distraction, no talking. I was a complete sponge, soaking up every word that came out of the instructor's mouth. We basically covered the entire Bible, even as far back as Abraham, when he was told to sacrifice his son Isaac. Then we combed through the books of the Old Testament and the New Testament. I found it all very interesting. The entire class consisted of about eight to nine people at a time. The school has continued until this present day. One of the students in my class was a doctor, she shared that she had delivered over five hundred babies in her career, another an architect from Mexico that had built buildings, a photographer, one a psychologist, and the rest were all professionals in their field. I was the only one without a title in front of my name. I was just a pastor's son. Yet, the Lord saw me fit to be in this class, at this school in Brazil.

Once the two weeks of training was complete, we were now going to travel three days into the Amazon jungle. I couldn't fathom just how big the Amazon jungle was until I drove into it. Toward the third day of traveling, we literally drove through the jungle the entire day, and I was told that we were nowhere near the end of it. We passed village after village, yet the jungle continued. At one point we had to stop at a checkpoint. We needed to show clearance just to get through because there was so much gold and precious metals in the land. We had to prove that we were there for religious reasons before we could continue. At times the jungle was so deep and dense that I was not able to walk one foot into it. I saw the pink dolphins that are exclusive only to the Amazon. The rivers and bodies of waters were so big that it was mind-blowing. Once we arrived, I felt as if I was in a national geographic documentary. Most of the indigenous were completely naked, it was a normal way of life for them.

When we exited the bus, we met the chief of a tribe. We learned very quickly that if you even slightly heavy-set, you are considered beautiful and rich. To them, being overweight meant that you had plenty to eat, which means wealth. As we gathered outside of the bus, the chief looks at me and pointed at the doctor and says, "I want her as my wife." I had to quickly step in and say she was my wife. We were trained to protect each other. He was the chief of the town and it made me a bit nervous. All around the town were indigenous people with no clothes on. The men looked like warriors very much like the movie *Apocalypto*. I was in a completely different world. Our mission was to minister to two specific tribes, not just about Christ, but to help them in any way they needed. Some of them wore shirts given to them by the missionaries, but none of them wore pants.

I was told by the missionaries that one of the tribes were cannibals just twenty years ago. This was when they first began ministering to them. Since then they've shared the gospel with them, fed them, and given them medical care. Being that I was from California, I am covered in tattoos.

I was a bit worried that the native people wouldn't know how to react to me. They didn't have tattoos. The most they had was ink that came from a plant. The women would mark themselves with it and it would last a week. Many of the natives were surprised that my tattoos wouldn't come off. One day we were going to go swimming with them. By this time, they hadn't seen all of the tattoos on my body. I was concerned that they would think I was evil or a witch doctor. But to my surprise, they didn't even give it a second glance. The lake was about twenty yards, and I could not believe how clear the water was. I could go underwater and open my eyes and see to the other side of the small lake. I noticed the natives were drinking the water, so I tried it and did not get sick.

I liked hanging around them, I was as curious of them as they were of me. They had bows and arrows and sticks. They would laugh at times, but usually, they were very quiet. I would hear them speak and couldn't grasp one single word. It was sounds I had never heard in all of my life. One bible verse sounded loud in my heart as I sat with the people.

Acts 1:8 nkjv – *But you shall receive power when the Holy Spirit has come upon you; and you shall be witnesses to Me in Jerusalem, and in all of Judea and Samaria, and to the end of the earth.*

Here I was, witnessing this very verse. To the ends of the earth. This was probably the furthest people on the planet, and I was seeing the power of God in the deepest parts of the Amazon jungle.

One of the leaders shared a story with us. Years ago, a

missionary dedicated his life to live with the indigenous people in the Amazon. His goal was to live with them for ten years to learn their language. He did not preach to them during all of this time. He wanted to be accepted and respected by them first. Once he learned the language, he began to translate the Bible into their dialect. Then one day he stood in front of them all and began to read it in their language. The people rushed to him and began ripping the pages and eating the paper. They believed that if they ate the pages, that God would live in them. It was their way of interpreting John1:1 nkjv.

In the beginning was the Word, and the Word was with God, and the Word was God.

I believe that God was working with their simple faith. The Lord was reaching their hearts. It was one of many stories that I was told about past missionaries.

Another story was of a missionary that would preach the gospel and tribes would walk hours to come to hear him. And after the preaching, they would leave a gift. They had no money, so they would leave a shirt, or beads or jewelry. It's a side of ministry that many never hear about. These things were not only happening in Brazil, but in Bolivia and other countries in South America.

One of the first meetings in the village, the chief had his men there. They began playing their flutes and doing witchcraft. We didn't want to interrupt them because it would be offensive. Yet, we were in prayer throughout their ceremony. We were praying for a circle of heavenly angels and for the Holy Spirit to cover us. We were trained to be in prayer against anything they were calling upon. This was complete, unhindered spiritual warfare.

When they were done, they invited us to do our thing. Someone from our team pulled out a guitar and we began worshiping Jesus. To them, it sounded like nice music, but Christ was in the midst of it all through the Holy Spirit. After a while, they started moving their hands in worship. It was beautiful. I had been in churches all my life, so I knew when the Holy Spirit would begin to move in the hearts of men and women. What surprised me, was out here. With a complete language barrier and no way to communicate. Yet I felt the Holy Spirit begin to move in their hearts. God is beyond language, beyond dialects. It was a powerful moment.

After two weeks of being out in the Amazon jungle, we were going to end it with a campaign. It was going to consist of food, ministry, and all the nearby tribes were invited. One thing I know is gang tension, and even out here I felt it. When two of the tribes showed up, I felt that familiar tension. I had to warn the missionaries and told them to watch a certain individual. There was something going on and we didn't know what, but I could smell it in the air. I didn't want anyone in danger.

After everyone had eaten, we were all ready to hear the preaching. I was very excited about this part. The man preaching would be Gustavo, the man in my dream. Sure enough, just like I saw in my vision, he arrived with his two black assistants. I didn't speak his language, and during the service, I couldn't understand him as he preached with an interpreter that translated into the local dialect. As he preached, I thought of the vision I received from God when I was in Colombia. Here I was in Brazil. I saw the red dirt and even kept some in a jar to take home. And I was about to have a few words with this man that told me to come to Brazil in my vision.

The service was done, and the team ministered to the people. The doctor was helping anyone that was sick, the photographer was taking photos, everyone was helping in whatever way they could. Gustavo was finally available for me to speak to him. He didn't speak English or Spanish, so I grabbed a translator. This was the moment I had waited for.

I walked up to him. Then through the translator, I introduced myself and began to share with him my vision in full detail. He listened intently.

I said, "I am here. You told me to come and here I am."

He reached over and laid hands on me. Then he began to pray in his language. I felt something like a warm blanket come over me. Like a piece of the kingdom right then and there. Everything else disappeared and nothing else mattered. I couldn't even understand what he was saying to me. There was a warmth from the inside coming out. Somehow, I felt like I was transforming and something was being deposited into me.

I know I've gone through struggles and life has hit me hard at times. Yet I knew from that moment on, I would never be the same again.

13

THE PROMISE

It was a beautiful sunny Sunday morning. The church that my dad pastored was full of people. The excitement was in the air as I sat in the pew wearing a suit. I never thought I would be in a place like this in my life. I looked over at my dad and he looked so proud. It all felt surreal. For so many years, my dad and I were going opposite directions. To be honest, I can't believe I survived the madness that the enemy dragged me through. My dad was behind the pulpit giving announcements. Even though he didn't look directly at me, I knew there was joy on his face. it was undeniable. Almost as if his entire posture had changed as well as his demeanor.

Even though I was gone to Brazil for a month, and six months in Colombia. It had been a lifetime to get to this point, right here right now. I know that my dad had wanted me to share with the congregation when I got back from Colombia. Due to my toothache, I didn't attend the mid-week service, and by the weekend I was gone to Brazil. At the time I regretted not being able to attend. But now as I sit here, I think the timing of God is always perfect.

My mind drifts off to the promise given to my dad when I was five years old. The vision that someday I would be in Colombia, in a white shirt, yelling out "*Colombia para Cristo!*" The journey was unbelievable even to me. Many times, we see someone in a church service. They might be crying or clapping or jumping up and down during worship. And we tend to think they are fake or exaggerating. Yet, we can never judge them. We have no idea what type of darkness or cave God brought them out of. That's why it's called salvation. We are saved from inevitable doom, we are saved from ourselves. We were headed straight to destruction by our own doing. Like a child innocently playing with string, then slowly getting tangled up within it. Then before they realize, it is too late to get themselves out. That is what so many of us need to realize and finally admit. To cry out to God and say, "Lord, please help me. I need you. I'm all tangled up and I can't break free." That prayer, those words are the essence of surrendering your life to Jesus. It does not have to be a fancy written out prayer. It is simply asking God to help you unwrap your life. "Lord open the door, break the chain, set me free."

I knew the moment was coming for my dad to ask me to share with the congregation all that had happened in the last few months. I realized this would be the very first time that I would share a pulpit with my dad. What an honor, to stand with such a God-fearing man. A man with so much faith and belief in God. That no matter what storms came, he stood like the palm tree. Swaying in the wind, but never toppling over. Even in my madness, I always had the desire to be a good pastor's son. To be a pastor or a leader. To follow in my dad's footsteps. To become something in the Kingdom of God, to work alongside my dad to further the gospel of Jesus Christ.

When my dad did call me up, there was no way I could talk about everything that was on my heart. I shared about the experience in Brazil. The church had a good time as I told them about the cannibal story, the Amazon jungle. I shared with them about the intense first two weeks in prayer and in the classroom. It was very hard to condense the last few months into a few minutes, but the people were loving the testimony. I also brought back thirty shirts from the school and sold them as an offering to send back to Brazil. I sold each one to help them at the Ambassador school. As I am writing this book, this is only the second time I've ever shared my life in this way.

After the service, like most typical Latino churches, we had a feast. So many people were coming up to talk to me, asking me questions about Colombia. I began sharing with some of them about my experience. I looked over at my dad and he looked back at me with pride. Not a false pride that leads to sin, but a Godly pride of a father for a son that he loves. I hardly ever saw that look from my dad toward me.

One time I will never forget, my dad approached me. I had been working hard and doing well at that time.

He said, "Son, I am more proud of you being my son, than me receiving my Ph.D."

I knew he meant it, and those words from him meant the world to me. Now here at his church, it was another of those special moments between us. It took a lot of courage for such a young man, newly in Christ to go out on my own in a foreign continent. Just with the belief in the vision my dad saw, and by the voice I heard when I stepped off the plane in Colombia. It is moments like this that I will engrave in my heart and take to my grave.

Finally, the food was served, and I sat down to eat. One of the elders of the church sat down with me to conversate, she was a prayer warrior. She was the type of woman that would pray for someone for hours, interceding for them. While talking to her, I could feel someone looking at me. I wasn't even looking in that direction, yet I knew. I couldn't hold back any longer, so I turned to see who was staring at me. It was a young lady named Esther. Her mom knew my parents and brought Esther along to hear my testimony. Even though they attended another church, they came to show support. After a few minutes, my mother walks over to Esther. She quickly glanced at her hand to see if she was wearing a wedding ring. My mom has always been the type to introduce people. When she saw that she wasn't wearing a ring, she brought her over to me.

"Do you remember her? This is Esther" she asked me.

"No," I answered.

"I have videos of both of you together when you were eight and nine years old. Her mom attended our church and you were in Sunday school with her."

Apparently, Esther and I were in the same children's class

when my dad was a young pastor and just starting out in ministry. I couldn't help but notice how attractive and beautiful she looked. Little did I know what the Lord was up to. Even though I wasn't in the mindset of having a relationship, in time Esther became my wife. I still joke with her about that day. I tell her that I felt her eyes shooting lasers at me as she checked me out. She denies it to this day and we laugh about it. I found out years later, that on that day my dad called some of his deacons up to his office within a half hour of me meeting Esther. He told them, "that young lady is going to be Alfonso's wife. Let's pray about it."

Eventually, I did marry her, and we now have a beautiful family with two sons, Xzavier who is nine and Josiah who is five years old at the time of this writing. I am thirty-eight years old and have been married to Esther for fourteen years so far.

As I said earlier, I have only shared my full testimony twice in public. But this is the only time I have shared my story in detail. I truly pray that it blesses all who read or hear my story. When I spoke at my dad's church, I only spoke about the Brazil experience. The only time I shared about Colombia in public was when I shared a small portion of it at House of Rest in Modesto. I wasn't fully prepared that day, so I did the best I could, and it is up on YouTube to this day. You can search it by looking up *(Testimony – brother Alfonso from House of Rest)*. I pray that it blesses you and encourages you. I also pray that it touches lives.

Epilogue

I miss the days when the pastor would give a prophetic Word of God to the people. It seems as if that type of ministry is going away. Back, decades ago or further back, the pastor would wack you with some Holy Word and deposit it into your life. I know that many of you have been given a Word. Maybe you were a child, or as an adult. Or even in reading the Bible, and God made something jump out at you. A promise that just locked into your heart and soul. A Word that God spoke over the purpose of your life. Maybe through your career or in your walk with Christ. I was one of those kids that eight out of ten times, the pastor would always give me a Word. There are people that haven't been given any Word spoken into their life. This is so important! Those words spoken into me were pieces of heaven, pieces of hope, pieces of a future. I needed those Words to hold me the way a string holds a kite. Without the string, the kite will just blow away any which way the wind desires, and after a moment, it will crash-dive down to the earth. Many of us are broken kites laying in a field, waiting for a Word to be tied to us so we can soar the way we were destined to. And the best part about it is, the kite string isn't being held by a pastor, but by Jesus Himself.

Anytime a pastor or evangelist would visit our church, I always knew a Word was coming my way. That is just the way I grew up. I know there are many of you just waiting for a Word. But God has spoken, through a bible study, through a sermon, through a loved one. We just need to go into a quiet place and remember back when a Word was spoken over your life. We need to entertain those things in our heart again, instead of the things our flesh wants us to entertain. Then when you remember those Words given to you, we need to add faith to those Words, until it comes to completion in your life. It will come alive in God's time. The Bible says that His Word does not come back void. That is a guarantee.

Isaiah 55:11 King James Version (KJV)

11 *So shall my word be that goeth forth out of my mouth: it shall not return unto me void, but it shall accomplish that which I please, and it shall prosper in the thing whereto I sent it.*

In my life, I have tried to rush things. Many times, I get in line for the race and don't wait for the gunshot to begin running. I just run without preparation. God wants us to prepare so many aspects of our life, in so many different areas. When we don't prepare, and the time comes for the Word given to us to come to life, we fail. Then we think God was wrong, or God failed. No! God never fails. We have failed to prepare. That is why many times we are Given a Word when we were young because God knew it was going to take a lifetime to prepare ourselves. For those reading this that have children. Do you speak a Word of God over their lives? Please, do not hold it in. They need to hear it, especially from you. Are you a pastor, a husband, a wife? The people you shepherd need to hear it. If they do not hear it, how can they prepare for it? By not giving them a Word that you are hearing from God over their lives, you are setting them up for failure. God wants to release those Words over our lives, but it is our responsibility to prepare ourselves. That way we can run this race and win. I once heard pastor David quote his mother when he was growing up. She would tell him, "Someday you will come to the Lord. Whether walking to Him or on your knees, you will come. Because I gave you to Him when you were a little boy." No matter what direction we choose in life, God's promises will follow us. If a Word is truly of God, it will happen.

I say all these things because of the promise God gave to my dad when I was five years old. I thank God that my dad didn't keep that promise in his heart. No! He immediately called me over and spoke it over me. And he never stopped speaking it over me. He would remind me all of the time.

I need to say something else that comes with the Word of God. This is also inevitable, so it must be talked about. The enemy knows when God is truly invoking a calling on a person. The enemy does not know the future, only God does. Yet, even though the enemy does not have insight into our future, he has studied man for centuries. When this vision was spoken into my life, I believe the enemy made plans to destroy my dad, destroy his faith and most of all destroy me. I know that everyone has stumbles and tragedy in their lives, but I truly believe that the things that happened to me don't happen to everyone. I feel as if the enemy has gone out of his way to trample and stomp this calling out of me. Yet despite every arrow, the enemy threw at me, the promise still came true. I came out of it with a lot of wounds, and if you could see my soul you would see the footprints all over me from the enemy. Yet, through it all, outshining every footprint, bruise, and scar, is the powerful, yet tender fingerprints of God.

This book is not about me. I did not write this for me. I already know my story. I wrote this for you, the reader. This book is about the promises that are going to reach you. Some of you need to be reminded of those promises. And even though many of you have those footprints of satan all over your soul. Trying to stomp out your marriage, your children, your life. I still say this over you, His promises will happen. In Jesus name, it will happen. No matter what, the devil cannot stop it. He might try to kill us and destroy us, but if it's a God thing, it will not be stopped.

When you come upon a field of grain, it is grown for the sole purpose to be made into bread, to give nutrition to the eater. Yet, it is impossible to grab a handful of grain and just begin chewing and eating it. It will destroy your teeth if you did that. First, the grain has to be ground down into powder. In the old days, a giant circular millstone was used to grind the grain. And only when it was powder, was it able to be used to make bread. Then the bread could be used to feed the people. I say all of that to say this. We were that grain, and life was the millstone that has broken us into powder. Yet, now that we are powder, God uses us to be bread for the world. Before Christ, we are in our broken state. When we surrender, it is us coming to His throne. And the beautiful part is, He doesn't leave us as a powder. Through His Word, he makes us into fresh bread.

Besides being bread for the world, you are also a fire. Remember, fire is used to shed light into darkness. The enemy would love to put your fire out. Especially if you have been called into ministry, evangelizing, preaching, teaching and reaching the lost. So if you have been given a Word, and you have been stomped on, rejoice. Because it simply means that God is going to catapult you to a place that you never imagined. It's okay to be in the line of fire. You can't be effective in war unless you are on the front line of the battle. I have heard it said, that salvation is free, but discipleship will cost you everything.

When you are in a church, or a study, or an outreach. Please keep the leaders in your prayers. Please realize that the enemy has declared war on anyone that speaks in the name of Jesus. We as the body of Christ, need to be alert to these things. The fire must stay lit no matter what. We did not choose God, He chose us. I urge you to keep your pastor and your leaders in prayer.

To put this entire book in a nutshell, I will summarize my thoughts with this. The Christian rapper Bryann Trejo says, "We are not here to share war stories. we are here to give God Glory." This sums it up well. I know there are situations in this book where in my past I thought I was someone cool. I want to set the record straight, I was not cool. I hated sharing the things I was involved with, it brings me shame. Yet I knew I had to share it, for you to know that there is a God and that God is bigger than the biggest sin. That no matter how lost I was, He still found me. And no matter how lost you might be, or someone you love, He will still find them. God is still in control. I hope I didn't waste your time with you thinking that this book is about me. If that is what you think then I failed. This book is not about me, it is about God. It is about how powerful He is. I pray that each page, each word in this book glorifies God. God's promises will happen in your life. May His fingerprints be upon all that you do. In Jesus name. Amen.

Philippians 1:6 (NIV)

⁶being confident of this, that he who began a good work in you will carry it on to completion until the day of Christ Jesus.

ALFONSO GOMEZ

The Lord Spoke, "Buy 36 chairs"

Dedication

First of all, I would like to dedicate this book to my wife Esther and my two boys, Xzavier and Josiah. I pray that my sons will one day finish the next chapters of this book. I would also like to take the time to honor my mom and dad. Also to honor God for this project. I come from a ministry family and am in no way trying to discredit the church with what I am about to say. Many times our childhood was hard due to my dad's dedication to God and the church, yet many times he was taken for granted. I know what organized church looks like behind closed doors. I know how administrators can act when they unhappily hand the pastor a check, or how deacons can be when they have hidden agendas. I've seen church politics from a different angle. It was ugly at times. This was in no way every church I grew up in. I also know it was not the church as a whole, it was individuals that had their hearts in the wrong place. This affected me greatly, yet my parents still stood strong and went through it. They never stopped and to this day have not stopped.

Mom, Dad. You did a great job. I appreciate your struggle and I love you. I know for a fact that you both have many footprints of the enemy on your souls. You were never cowards and took the beating. You embraced the cost, and now the fingerprints of God is evident in your lives.

Thank You

These are the first two copies #1 & #2 of the book God's Fingerprints – Story of a Pastor's Son. I want to take a moment to thank Pastor David Rocha of House of Rest Church. Thank you for helping me tell my story, and for having the talent to project the message that the Lord is showing the world through this book. It's not about me, it's about God. I am very proud of the outcome. I could not have accomplished without you. May God bless you in bringing the mission of telling so many stories and testimonies through your authoring and publishing in the future. Let the revolution begin, all glory to God.

Thank you, Alfonso Gomez

FUTURE RELEASES
Lost in the Storm By Pastor David Rocha

Other future titles:
The Kingdom of God
Always With You – novel
Who Are You – Identity teaching
To contact author Alfonso Gomez
Email: alfonsoluis_gomez@hotmail.com
to contact Author David Rocha
Email: houseofrestchurch@gmail.com
www.houseofrestchurch.com

To contact author Alfonso Gomez
Email: alfonsoluis_gomez@hotmail.com
to contact Author David Rocha
Email: houseofrestchurch@gmail.com
www.houseofrestchurch.com

www.ingramcontent.com/pod-product-compliance
Lightning Source LLC
Chambersburg PA
CBHW052057070526
44584CB00017B/2219